QUICK FIXES
WITH CAKE MIXES

Cakes
Cookies
Bars
Goodies

Great Tasting Desserts Made With Mixes

By
Lia Roessner Wilson

Published By
Cookbook Resources, LLC
Highland Village, Texas

QUICK FIXES
WITH CAKE MIXES

Cakes ◆ Cookies ◆ Bars ◆ Goodies
Great Tasting Desserts Made With Mixes

1st Printing	2001
2nd Printing	2002
3rd Printing	2002
4th Printing	2003
5th Printing	2004
6th Printing	2005
7th Printing	2005
8th Printing	2006

ISBN 1-931294-88-7 (hardcover)
Library of Congress Number 2004117143
ISBN 1-931294-28-3 (papercover)
Library of Congress Number 2004117144

Illustrations by Nancy Murphy Griffith
Typesetting by Fit to Print, Inc. Dallas, Texas

Designed, Printed, Published and Manufactured in the
United States of America by
Cookbook Resources, LLC
541 Doubletree Drive
Highland Village, Texas 75077
Toll free 866-229-2665
www.cookbookresources.com

cookbook
resources LLC

INTRODUCTION

My experiences with cake mixes go way back. They've always come in handy when I've made decorated cakes because they were such a timesaver. In addition to being moist, they tasted good and made a great base for my decorating. Instead of spending time making a cake from scratch, I'd pop a cake in the oven made from a mix and then focus my time and energy on the icing and the decorations.

I then learned that they were useful not only as a "canvas" for my cake decorating, but also as a base for some really good desserts. I could add some ingredients to them and take a cake to a new level, like **Cool and Fruity Lemon Cake** on page 22. This will be a hit for you in the summertime or use them to make bar cookies, like **Pecan Pie Bars** on page 174. These bars are just like a pie, but more fun because you eat them with your hands! Cake mixes can even be used to make cookies. You'll be amazed how fast you can create a big batch of drop cookies using a mix and a few other ingredients.

In addition to **altering cake mixes to make cookies,** I figured that I could **do the same with a cookie mix**, so I started experimenting, mainly with sugar cookie mixes, to see what kinds of creations could be made. It's amazing what assortment of cookie tastes and styles can be made from a simple mix! I'm excited to be able to include some really cool cookie recipes in this book, such as **Chocolate-Dipped Malted Milk Cookies**, page 167, and a variety of sandwich cookies that reflect the holiday seasons, page 156. One of my all-time favorites, **Ginger Jam Sandwich Cookies**, page 160, has the wonderful flavor of ginger combined with jam in a pretty little cookie that you'd never guess was made from a sugar cookie mix. All of these can be made faster than you can say, "Please hand me that mix"!

I hope you have fun with all of the recipes included in this book. They are a cinch to make and I'm sure that there's going to be a favorite for everyone in your house. When you do find one that you particularly like, you can write it down in the handy Personal Record on page 18. Use the index to keep track of your favorite recipes by page, as well as write any special information you want to be sure to remember.

Happy baking!
Lia

CONTENTS

You'll find cakes of all kinds: including everything from a Bundt cake that requires no icing to a tiered torte complete with filling and frosting to sheet cakes you simply bake, frost and serve out of the same pan. With a few additional ingredients or an extra step or two, you can create good-looking and really tasty treats. It's all just a breeze, really!

You'll be amazed at the wide range of cookie styles and flavors you can create by using a cookie mix or cake mix as a base. The only thing more gratifying than making them is hearing the delighted squeals from family and friends who will not believe they were made from a mix! And they're all just a snap!

CONTENTS

BAKER'S TOOLS

(Fun Surprises You Can Give Yourself!)

You've got to have a spoon, a bowl and a cake pan, but there are a few other baking tools that aren't real necessities until you see how much fun and easy they make baking. Give yourself a special baking tool tomorrow and have a great time!

CAKE PANS
For stacked layer cakes, round pans are the best.

BUNDT CAKE PAN
One-pan cakes look great with or without icing.

CAKE TESTER
Sometimes a toothpick just won't do.

ZESTER
Make grating a breeze with this handy tool and cleanup is easier too.

CAKE SLICER
Get nice, flat tops
and perfectly even layers.

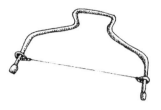

SILICONE SPATULAS
Get every bit of that icing
or cake batter out of the bowl.

SKEWER
Another great way to test for doneness, a skewer is perfect
for testing the deep Bundt cakes.

ELECTRIC MIXER
Once you try it,
you won't give it up.

WIRE WHISK
Bye, bye lumps.

JUICER
Quickly and cleanly gets
all the juice out of the fruit.

EASY TIPS

Following these few simple tips can help you bake better cakes—and make your life less stressful!

♦ **TURN UP THE HEAT**
Don't forget to preheat your oven to the required temperature before you begin mixing ingredients. When you're ready to pop your cake in the oven, you don't have to wait for it to heat to the proper temperature.

♦ **GET CENTERED**
Bake your cakes on the center rack of your oven. When using two pans (for layer cakes, for instance), position them in the middle of the oven and don't let them touch each other or the sides of the oven.

♦ **COOL IT**
Cool your cake in the pan after removing it from the oven for about 10 to 15 minutes (unless the recipe specifies otherwise), before turning it out onto a cooling rack.

♦ **DON'T GET STUCK**
Grease and flour your pans—unless the recipe specifies otherwise. If you're not using an all-purpose baking spray for cake pans, then grease them first using a small piece of wax paper or plastic wrap and a tablespoon of shortening and dust lightly with flour (about a teaspoon or two). Shake the flour over the inside to coat and dump out. If you see any shiny spots, coat and flour them before baking the cake.

♦ Use cocoa to "flour" a pan for a chocolate cake to avoid the unsightly look of browned flour contrasted against the dark cake.

TEST YOUR CAKE FOR DONENESS

There are a couple of methods for testing your cake toward the end of baking time to be sure it's completely baked before you pull it out of the oven.

The most reliable, I think, is using a cake tester (which can be a toothpick, bamboo skewer or tool created for this purpose) inserted into the center of the cake.

If it comes out clean (or with only a few crumbs attached) your cake is finished. If it comes out with batter on it, you need to leave the cake in for a few minutes more and test again.

You can also lightly press the cake surface with your finger. If the cake springs back it's cooked.

ADD "ZEST" TO YOUR CAKES WITH GRATED FRUIT RIND

One of the best ways to add citrus flavor to your cakes is with grated fruit rind (like orange, lemon, or lime). Several recipes in this book call for "lemon zest" or "orange zest" and there are a couple of things to keep in mind when using this ingredient.

◆ Only use colored part of the rind, not the pith (the white part), which can be bitter.

◆ Grate the rind against the rough side of a grater over a piece of wax paper. When you're finished grating, you can gently lift the wax paper, fold it slightly and shake the zest into your measuring tool.

BRING OUT THE FLAVORS OF NUTS

The flavors of pecans, almonds, walnuts and pine nuts are enhanced when they are toasted. To toast nuts, spread them on baking sheet, bake at 275° (135° C) for about 5 minutes and remove from oven. Try a "before-and-after" taste test to see for yourself.

LIQUID GLAZES

Several recipes in this book call for poking holes in a baked cake, over which you then pour a liquid glaze. The most effective method I've found for doing this (since many of the cakes that call for this technique are deep pans) is to use bamboo skewers, which you can easily find in the baking section or Asian foods section of your grocery store. There are several reasons for this.

◆ They are just the right diameter for making holes large enough to absorb the icing, without damaging the surface of the cake.

◆ They also are easy on coated pans. You don't want to use a utensil that's going to gouge or scratch a non-stick surface.

◆ They are inexpensive and disposable, although if you want to, you can wash them and reuse.

◆ They are long enough to reach the center of a bundt cake where a toothpick won't reach.

TIMESAVERS

Using a mix as the basis for your dessert is the first step to saving time; however, there are some other things you can do to shave off a few minutes here or there. It may not sound like a lot of time, but when you add them up, they can really make a difference.

◆ Make liberal use of the microwave when it comes to softening ingredients like chocolate, butter or cream cheese.

Set the microwave cooking temperature on defrost for short cooking times (like 30 to 45 seconds at a time) and check each time to make sure that the ingredient is becoming soft without melting or cooking.

◆ Grease and flour your pans! My favorite way to grease and flour a cake pan is to use an all-purpose baking spray designed for greasing pans. Not only is this fast, but it's less messy than using the traditional 2-step method of using shortening and flour.

If you're using a pan with decorative sides (like a bundt pan), the spray also easily coats the indentations that are difficult to cover when coating by hand.

◆ Make your cake ahead of time—If you know you're going to need or want a cake on a certain day, bake it a couple of days in advance and refrigerate or freeze it. (Cakes can be wrapped and frozen for up to three months in advance. Wrap them first in plastic wrap and then foil.)

When you're ready to use it, pull it out of the freezer, let it thaw and then frost it.

◆ Make your icing ahead of time and refrigerate it until you're ready to use it to keep it fresh. Just warm it to room temperature before using.

◆ Most important of all, check your list of ingredients ahead of time to be sure you have everything you need!

I've made countless last-minute dashes to the store in the middle of baking a cake because I was missing an essential ingredient.

LOOK LIKE A PRO

It wasn't until I took a cake decorating course that I realized what kinds of tools and supplies were readily available for making homemade cakes look great. I was thrilled to find the *cake slicer*—no more miscalculated attempts to cut the domed top off a cake evenly with a knife. And the *cake boxes* were a real find.

There's nothing worse than putting the finishing touches on a lovely cake you plan to take to a get-together only to find you then have no container to put it in for easy transport.

Your local hobby store carries a range of supplies, including cake boxes, cake boards, cake slicer, pans and decorating tools. I keep a stash of cake boards on hand in several sizes—both round and rectangular.

Although you can purchase decorative foil to cover the boards, I generally use aluminum foil. I wrap the board carefully and then tape the foil down on the back. You can then put your cake directly on this and if you want, in a box. The boxes come flat and unassembled. They're wonderful for protecting your cake and making it easy to carry.

Cake Slicer

Slice your cakes neatly and easily with a cake slicer. I bought mine for about $3.00—a very worthwhile investment for getting trim, even layers.

ICING SPATULA

An icing spatula makes icing a cake much easier! You can get a really nice, smooth finish not only on the top, but also on the sides.

CAKE BOARD

Often it's difficult to find a plate large and flat enough to accommodate a cake, so a cake board is a functional (disposable) solution.

FOIL FOR COVERING BOARD

Since your cake's appearance won't be enhanced by the bare cardboard cake board, you can cover it with aluminum foil (which I frequently do) for a nice surface. What looks even better, however, is the gold foil designed specifically for this purpose. It looks very nice beneath the cake and is easy to apply to the board. You simply cover the board and tape the edges underneath.

DOILY

If you don't want to use foil, or even if you do, a lacy doily peeking out from beneath your cake can really be a dressy finishing touch.

SPECIAL TOUCHES

There are a few simple things that you can do on your own to add some flair to your cakes and cookies. They're much easier to do than you would think.

COLORED SUGAR TO JAZZ UP CAKES AND COOKIES

You can easily make your own colored sugar to use on cookies and cakes by adding a few drops of food color to granulated sugar and mix well until all the sugar is coated. Add 2 drops to ¼ cup (60 mL) sugar.

CANDIED PECANS:

1 EGG WHITE	**1**
1 TABLESPOON WATER	**15 ML**
½ CUP PACKED BROWN SUGAR	**125 ML**
2 CUPS PECAN HALVES	**500 ML**

◆ Preheat oven to 300° (149° C). Grease a cookie sheet or baking pan with a low rim. In medium bowl, beat egg white and water until foamy. Add brown sugar; stir until sugar dissolves. Stir in pecan halves until well coated. Pour pecan mixture onto cookie sheet (some of the sugar mixture will flow out from around the pecans; thus the reason for the rimmed baking pan).

◆ Bake until nuts are brown and crisp (about 25 minutes). Stir every 10 minutes or so and scoop the sugar mixture onto pecans as you stir.

◆ Remove from oven and stir to loosen nuts from cookie sheet and separate from each other. Cool completely and store in an airtight container at room temperature. The candied nuts will keep for days if you store them like this.

CHOCOLATE LEAVES

Few finishing touches look more stunning on a cake than leaves made out of chocolate. They're unbelievably easy to make and take nothing more than some chocolate, a cheap paintbrush (like the kind that comes with a water color set) and some non-toxic leaves from a bush or tree.

♦ To make about 12 medium-size leaves, first wash and thoroughly dry your leaves. Take a 1-ounce (28 g) square of chocolate and melt it. (I do this in the microwave; see tip in Timesavers section.) Dip your paintbrush into the chocolate, hold the leaf by the stem (try to leave a stem on it for this purpose) and paint a thick layer of chocolate on the back. Work in small sections, dipping your brush in the chocolate as necessary, until the entire back is coated. You can wait a few minutes and add a second coat. (You want the chocolate to be somewhat thick, so when you peel the leaf away it will be substantial enough to keep its form without breaking.)

♦ Do this for as many leaves as you need and place them on wax paper to cool and to harden. (I put them in the refrigerator to speed the process.)

♦ Once cool, carefully peel the leaves away. (Try not to touch the chocolate with your hands, because they will melt. Use a toothpick to hold the chocolate as you peel the leaf.)

♦ I've found that leaves with some flexibility work well. If they are too stiff, the chocolate breaks when you peel the leaf away. (Rose bush leaves work great. They are just the right size and keep their shape when coated.)

17

MY PERSONAL RECORD

Page #	Recipe Name	Comments

It's A Breeze . . .

When it comes to baking, crafts or other hobbies, everything you make is created in steps. I'm always amazed that what appears to be difficult is really much easier than I thought if I just take it step by step.

Nothing here is difficult, so just take these cake recipes step by step and you will love the time you save and the rewards you earn.

And remember, it's all a breeze!

Sheet Cakes, Bundt Cakes, Layer Cakes, Tortes and Special Cakes

Sheet cakes, bundt cakes, layer cakes and tortes! You'll find cakes of all kinds in this section, including everything from a bundt cake that requires no icing at all to a four-tiered torte complete with filling and frosting. There are even recipes for pastries created with cake mixes.

The versatility of the cake recipes located on the following pages makes it easy to find a cake for any occasion and for almost any pan. The multi-layered tortes provide the opportunity to go all-out and create a really stunning, towering cake with a little extra effort, as well as the flexibility to create a simple two-layered cake by leaving out the filling between the sliced layers.

Sheet cakes couldn't be any easier. Simply bake and frost, then serve out of the same pan. But don't be fooled by their simplicity. With a few additional ingredients or an extra step or two, you can create good-looking, delightfully tasty treats.

APPLESAUCE CAKE
WITH PRALINE TOPPING

½ CUP BUTTER	125 ML
¼ CUP HEAVY CREAM	60 ML
1 CUP PACKED BROWN SUGAR	250 ML
1 ½ TO 2 CUPS PECAN HALVES	375 TO
	500 ML
1 (18 OUNCE) YELLOW CAKE MIX	1 (520 G)
1 CUP APPLESAUCE	250 ML
3 EGGS	3
½ CUP MILK	125 ML
⅓ CUP VEGETABLE OIL	80 ML

◆ Preheat oven to 325° (163° C). In medium saucepan, combine butter, cream and brown sugar. Cook over low heat, stirring occasionally, until butter melts and sugar dissolves.

◆ Pour mixture into well-greased 9 x 13-inch (23 x 33 cm) baking dish. Sprinkle enough pecans to cover the bottom of pan in a single layer.

◆ In large bowl, combine cake mix, applesauce, eggs, milk and oil. Beat on low speed to blend, then beat on medium speed for 2 to 3 minutes. Carefully pour batter evenly over pecan mixture. If necessary, very gently smooth top of batter to cover exposed pecan mixture.

◆ Bake for 40 to 45 minutes or until cake top springs back when lightly touched. Remove from oven and cool for 5 minutes. Turn cake out of pan onto serving tray. Let pan remain in place for 1 minute and then remove. If any praline topping sticks to inside of pan, just scrape it off and slap it back on the cake.

COOL AND FRUITY LEMON CAKE

You can use almost any fruit you like on this cake.
Depending on what's in season, the fruit topping can be
varied to suit your taste and what's in good supply at the
time. Try exotic fruits like mangoes and star fruits for a
unique taste experience and interesting presentation.

1 (18 OUNCE) YELLOW CAKE MIX	1 (520 G)
3 EGGS	3
1/3 CUP VEGETABLE OIL	80 ML
1 CUP MILK	250 ML
1/4 CUP LEMON JUICE	60 ML
1 TABLESPOON LEMON ZEST	15 ML

◆ Preheat oven to 350° (176° C). In large bowl, combine cake mix, eggs, oil, milk, lemon juice and lemon zest. Beat on low speed to blend, then beat on medium for 2 to 3 minutes.

◆ Pour batter into greased, floured 9 x 13-inch (23 x 33 cm) baking dish and bake for 30 to 35 minutes or until cake tester comes out clean.

◆ While cake is hot from the oven, poke holes 1/2 inch apart over entire cake surface and pour **Lemon Glaze** (page 23) evenly over top. Cool, smooth **Whipped Topping** (page 23) over top and cover with fresh fruit. (Slice fruit into 1/4 inch thick slices and arrange attractively over topping.)

Lemon zest is grated peel from citrus. See page 10.

(CONTINUED ON NEXT PAGE.)

(CONTINUED)

LEMON GLAZE:

2 CUPS POWDERED SUGAR	**500 ML**
JUICE FROM 2 MEDIUM LEMONS	**2**
ZEST FROM 2 MEDIUM LEMONS	**2**
1 TEASPOON ORANGE EXTRACT	**5 ML**

◆ In medium bowl, combine sugar, lemon juice, lemon zest and orange extract. Stir until they blend well.

WHIPPED TOPPING:

1 (14 OUNCE) CAN SWEETENED CONDENSED MILK	**1 (420 G)**
⅓ CUP FRESH LEMON JUICE	**80 ML**
ZEST OF 1 LEMON	**1**
4 OUNCES FROZEN WHIPPED TOPPING, THAWED	**115 G**

◆ In small bowl combine condensed milk, lemon juice and lemon zest, blend well and fold in whipped topping.

FRUIT:

2 KIWIS, SLICED	**2**
1 BANANA, SLICED	**1**
1 PINT STRAWBERRIES, SLICED	**1**

◆ Sprinkle banana slices with lemon juice or Fruit Fresh.

I like to slice the fruit, arrange kiwis in the middle, fan strawberries out on either side, place a row of bananas and kiwis and end with strawberries for a starburst effect.

FLUFFY ORANGE CAKE

This chilly dessert is a refreshing way to cool down on a hot summer day. If you don't have time to freeze it, don't worry. You can simply make it in time to refrigerate and serve it cool. You may actually prefer it this way.

1 (3 OUNCE) PACKAGE ORANGE GELATIN	1 (85 G)
1 CUP HOT WATER	250 ML
1 (18 OUNCE) YELLOW CAKE MIX	1 (520 G)
4 EGGS	4
⅔ CUP VEGETABLE OIL	160 ML
1 (8 OUNCE) PACKAGE CREAM CHEESE, SOFTENED	1 (228 G)
1 (14 OUNCE) CAN SWEETENED CONDENSED MILK	1 (420 G)
⅓ CUP FRESH LEMON JUICE	80 ML
1 (12 OUNCE) CONTAINER FROZEN WHIPPED TOPPING, THAWED	1 (340 G)
2 (11 OUNCE) CANS MANDARIN ORANGE SEGMENTS, DRAINED, HALVED	2 (312 G)

◆ Preheat oven to 350° (176° C). In small bowl, stir gelatin into hot water until it dissolves. In large bowl, combine cake mix, eggs, vegetable oil and gelatin mixture. Beat on low speed to blend, then beat on medium for 2 minutes.

◆ Pour batter into greased, floured 9 x 13-inch (23 x 33 cm) baking dish. Bake for 35 to 40 minutes or until cake tester comes out clean. Remove cake from oven and cool.

◆ **Prepare topping:** In large bowl, blend cream cheese and condensed milk until smooth. Stir in lemon juice and mix well. Fold in whipped topping until it blends. Fold in orange segments.

◆ Pour mixture over cooled cake and spread over top. Cover and freeze until 1 hour before serving.

BANANA-PINEAPPLE CAKE WITH BROILED COCONUT FROSTING

Delicious! This cake's light and delicate flavor complements the coconut frosting and isn't too sweet or rich.

1 (18 OUNCE) WHITE CAKE MIX	**1 (520 G)**
1 (8 OUNCE) CAN CRUSHED PINEAPPLE WITH JUICE	**1 (228 G)**
½ CUP MILK	**125 ML**
3 EGGS	**3**
3 TABLESPOONS VEGETABLE OIL	**45 ML**
1 CUP MASHED BANANAS	
(ABOUT 2 TO 3 MEDIUM BANANAS)	**250 ML**

◆ Preheat oven to 350° (176° C). In large bowl, combine cake mix, pineapple with juice, milk, eggs and oil. Beat on low speed to blend, about 1 minute.

◆ Add bananas and beat on medium speed for 2 minutes.

Pour batter into greased, floured 9 x 13-inch (23 x 33 cm) baking dish. Bake for 30 to 35 minutes or until cake browns lightly and tests done. During last 5 minutes of baking, prepare frosting. Frost the cake while it's hot from the oven.

BROILED COCONUT FROSTING:

¾ CUP PACKED BROWN SUGAR	**180 ML**
⅓ CUP (5 ⅓ TABLESPOONS) BUTTER	**80 ML**
2 TABLESPOONS MILK	**30 ML**
1 CUP SHREDDED COCONUT	**250 ML**
½ CUP CHOPPED PECANS	**125 ML**

◆ In medium saucepan, cook brown sugar, butter and milk over low to medium heat for 2 minutes or until butter melts. Remove from heat and stir in coconut and pecans.

◆ Set oven temperature to broil. Spread mixture over hot cake and return cake to oven for 2 to 3 minutes or until light brown on top. (Watch carefully so frosting will not burn; check after 1½ minutes.)

CHOCOLATE-OATMEAL CAKE

1 ½ CUPS BOILING WATER	375 ML
1 CUP QUICK-COOKING OATS	250 ML
1 CUP SEMI-SWEET CHOCOLATE CHIPS	250 ML
1 (18 OUNCE) WHITE CAKE MIX	1 (520 G)
¼ CUP (½ STICK) BUTTER, SOFTENED	60 ML
¼ CUP PACKED BROWN SUGAR	60 ML
3 EGGS	3

◆ Preheat oven to 325° (163° C). In small bowl, combine water and oats. Sprinkle chocolate chips over top (do not stir) and let stand for 20 minutes.

◆ In large bowl, combine cake mix, butter, brown sugar and eggs and beat on low speed to blend. Add oat mixture and beat on medium speed for 1 minute.

◆ Pour batter into greased, floured 9 x 13-inch (23 x 33) baking dish and bake for 35 to 40 minutes or until cake tester comes out clean. Cool and frost with *Coffee Frosting*.

COFFEE FROSTING:

2 TEASPOONS INSTANT COFFEE GRANULES	10 ML
3 TABLESPOONS HALF-AND-HALF, WARMED	45 ML
½ CUP (1 STICK) BUTTER, SOFTENED	125 ML
1 TEASPOON VANILLA EXTRACT	5 ML
PINCH SALT	
4 CUPS POWDERED SUGAR	1 L

◆ In small bowl, dissolve coffee granules in half-and-half. Set aside.

◆ In medium bowl, cream butter with vanilla and salt. Gradually beat in powdered sugar. Add coffee mixture and beat well. (If necessary, add small amounts of powdered sugar until frosting reaches spreading consistency.)

LEMON CREAM CHEESE SWIRL CAKE

⅓ CUP SUGAR	80 ML
1 (8 OUNCE) PACKAGE CREAM CHEESE, SOFTENED	1 (228 G)
4 EGGS, DIVIDED	4
1 TEASPOON LEMON EXTRACT	5 ML
1 (18 OUNCE) LEMON CAKE MIX WITH PUDDING	1 (520 G)
1 ¼ CUPS BUTTERMILK	310 ML
⅓ CUP VEGETABLE OIL	80 ML

◆ Preheat oven to 350° (176° C). In medium bowl, cream sugar and cheese until they blend well. Beat in 1 egg and lemon extract until mixture is light and fluffy. Set aside.

◆ In large bowl, combine cake mix with buttermilk, oil and 3 eggs. Beat on low speed for 2 to 3 minutes.

◆ Pour batter into greased, floured 9 x 13-inch (23 x 33 cm) baking dish. Pour cream cheese mixture on top of batter in 2 rows the length of the pan. Swirl cream cheese mixture through batter gently with a knife or spatula and be careful not to over mix. Bake for 30 to 35 minutes or until cake tester comes out clean. Cool and frost with *Lemon Icing*.

LEMON ICING:	
1 TEASPOON LEMON ZEST	5 ML
6 TABLESPOONS (¾ STICK) BUTTER, SOFTENED	90 ML
3 CUPS POWDERED SUGAR	750 ML
¼ CUP FRESH LEMON JUICE	60 ML

◆ In medium bowl, cream lemon zest and butter until they blend well. Add 1 cup (250 mL) powdered sugar and blend until completely incorporated.

◆ Add lemon juice and remaining sugar alternately and blend well after each addition until icing is smooth and reaches frosting consistency.

Lemon zest is grated peel from citrus. See page 10.

STRAWBERRY-LEMON CAKE WITH FLUFFY CREAM CHEESE FROSTING

This cake combines the tartness of lemons with the sweetness of strawberries. When you make it, you'll want to put the sliced strawberries on top just before serving to keep the juice from the strawberries from seeping into the icing and discoloring it.

1 (18 OUNCE) WHITE CAKE MIX	**1 (520 G)**
1 (3 OUNCE) PACKAGE LEMON GELATIN	**1 (85 G)**
1 ⅓ CUPS FROZEN STRAWBERRIES IN SYRUP,	
THAWED	**330 ML**
¼ CUP VEGETABLE OIL	**60 ML**
3 EGGS	**3**

◆ Preheat oven to 350° (176° C). In large bowl, combine cake mix, gelatin, strawberries in syrup, oil and eggs. Beat on low speed until they blend and beat on medium for 2 minutes. Pour batter into greased, floured 9 x 13-inch (23 x 33 cm) baking dish and bake for 35 minutes or until cake tester comes out clean. Cool and frost with *Fluffy Cream Cheese Frosting*.

FLUFFY CREAM CHEESE FROSTING:

4 OUNCES CREAM CHEESE, SOFTENED	**115 G**
¾ CUP SUGAR	**180 ML**
4 OUNCES FROZEN WHIPPED TOPPING, THAWED	**115 G**
1 (8 OUNCE) CONTAINER FRESH STRAWBERRIES,	
SLICED	**1 (228 G)**

◆ In large bowl, beat cream cheese and sugar until light and fluffy. Fold in whipped topping until they blend thoroughly. Frost cake and arrange sliced strawberries attractively on surface for decoration.

BANANA-NUT CAKE

1 (18 OUNCE) YELLOW CAKE MIX	**1 (520 G)**
3 EGGS	**3**
⅓ CUP VEGETABLE OIL	**80 ML**
1 CUP MILK	**250 ML**
3 TABLESPOONS SUGAR	**45 ML**
1 CUP MASHED RIPE BANANAS	
(ABOUT 2½ MEDIUM BANANAS)	**250 ML**
1 CUP CHOPPED BLACK WALNUTS	**250 ML**

◆ Preheat oven to 350° (176° C). In large bowl, combine cake mix, eggs, oil, milk and sugar. Beat on low speed to blend, beat on medium for 2 minutes.

◆ Add bananas and beat 1 more minute on medium. Stir in walnuts.

◆ Pour batter into greased, floured 9 x 13-inch (23 x 33 cm) baking dish. Bake for 30 to 35 minutes or until cake tester comes out clean. Let cake cool until just warm to the touch and spoon *Dark Caramel Glaze* over top.

DARK CARAMEL GLAZE:

1 CUP PACKED DARK BROWN SUGAR	**250 ML**
⅓ CUP HALF-AND-HALF CREAM	**80 ML**
¼ CUP (½ STICK) BUTTER	**60 ML**
1 TEASPOON VANILLA	**5 ML**

◆ In medium saucepan, melt brown sugar, half-and-half and butter over medium heat and bring to a boil. Boil for 6 minutes, stirring constantly until mixture thickens. Remove from heat and beat in vanilla.

◆ Spoon over warm cake as evenly as possible. To ensure adequate coverage, poke holes in top of cake with a toothpick or bamboo skewer before spooning glaze over top.

The glaze will have the consistency of a thick syrup.

7-UP CAKE

1 (18 OUNCE) LEMON CAKE MIX	1 (520 G)
1 (3 OUNCE) PACKAGE VANILLA	
INSTANT PUDDING	1 (85 G)
1 (8 OUNCE) CAN CRUSHED PINEAPPLE, DRAINED	1 (228 G)
1 CUP 7-UP	250 ML
⅔ CUP VEGETABLE OIL	160 ML
4 EGGS	4

◆ Preheat oven to 350° (176° C). In large bowl, combine cake mix, pudding mix, pineapple, 7-Up, oil and eggs. Beat on low speed to blend, then beat on medium for 3 minutes.

◆ Pour into greased, floured 9 x 13-inch (23 x 33 cm) baking dish. Bake for 30 to 35 minutes or until cake tester comes out clean. Cool and frost with *Coconut-Pineapple Frosting*.

COCONUT-PINEAPPLE FROSTING:

½ CUP (1 STICK) BUTTER	125 ML
1 ½ CUPS SUGAR	375 ML
1 (8 OUNCE) CAN CRUSHED PINEAPPLE	
WITH JUICE	1 (228 G)
2 TABLESPOONS FLOUR	30 ML
2 EGGS, SLIGHTLY BEATEN	2
1 CUP SHREDDED COCONUT	250 ML

◆ In medium saucepan, cook butter, sugar, pineapple with juice, flour and eggs over low to medium heat until they thicken.

◆ Remove from heat, stir in coconut and mix well. Spread over cake while still warm.

CINNAMON-BUN CAKE

1 (18 OUNCE) BUTTER RECIPE GOLDEN CAKE MIX	1 (520 G)
¾ CUP (1 ½ STICKS) BUTTER, MELTED	180 ML
4 EGGS	4
1 (8 OUNCE) CONTAINER SOUR CREAM	1 (228 G)
1 CUP PACKED LIGHT BROWN SUGAR	250 ML
1 TABLESPOON CINNAMON	15 ML

◆ Preheat oven to 325° (163° C). In medium bowl, beat cake mix, butter, eggs and sour cream on low speed for approximately 1 minute to blend. Pour half the batter into ungreased 9 x 13-inch (23 x 33 cm) baking dish.

◆ In small bowl, combine brown sugar and cinnamon and sprinkle over batter.

◆ Pour remaining batter over sugar mixture and swirl sugar mixture in cinnamon-bun design with a knife or spatula.

◆ Bake for 40 minutes. Soon after removing from oven, while cake is still hot, ice with *Powdered Sugar Glaze.*

POWDERED SUGAR GLAZE:	
2 CUPS POWDERED SUGAR	520 ML
4 TABLESPOONS MILK	60 ML
½ TEASPOON VANILLA EXTRACT	2 ML
½ TEASPOON BUTTER EXTRACT	2 ML

◆ In small bowl, mix powdered sugar, milk, vanilla and butter extract until they blend well.

CARAMEL-RIBBON PEAR CAKE

I sent this cake to work with my husband to get feedback.
The verdict came in: it was a keeper. Everyone loved the
moist texture of the pear-studded cake and the flavor
added by the caramel ribbon running through its middle.

1 CUP (2 STICKS) BUTTER, DIVIDED	250 ML
1 (18 OUNCE) SPICE CAKE MIX	1 (520 G)
1 (15 OUNCE) CAN PEARS IN HEAVY SYRUP	
WITH SYRUP	1 (438 G)
3 EGGS	3
1 (14 OUNCE) PACKAGE INDIVIDUALLY-WRAPPED	
CARAMELS (ABOUT 40 PIECES)	1 (420 G)
½ CUP EVAPORATED MILK	125 ML
1 ½ CUPS CHOPPED PECANS, DIVIDED	375 ML
¾ CUP PACKED BROWN SUGAR	180 ML

◆ Preheat oven to 350° (176° C). Melt ½ cup (1 stick) (125 mL)
butter and pour into large bowl. Add cake mix, 1 cup (250 mL)
pear syrup and eggs.

(CONTINUED ON NEXT PAGE.)

(CONTINUED)

◆ Beat on low speed to blend, then beat on medium for 2 minutes. Cut pears in half and stir into batter.

◆ Pour half of batter in greased, floured 9 x 13-inch (23 x 33 cm) baking dish. Bake for 15 minutes or until top of cake is "set".

◆ While cake is baking, prepare caramel. Combine remaining butter, caramels and milk in medium saucepan over low heat. Stir constantly until caramels melt and mixture is smooth.

◆ Pour over baked cake. Sprinkle ¾ cup (180 mL) pecans over top and add remaining cake batter.

◆ Combine brown sugar and remaining pecans. Sprinkle evenly over batter and return cake to oven for another 35 to 40 minutes or until cake tester comes out clean. Remove from oven and cool.

HONEY-CITRUS CAKE WITH LEMON GLAZE

With a delicate flavor and the sweetness of honey, this cake makes the perfect light dessert for a summer get-together or brunch.

1 (18 OUNCE) BUTTER RECIPE GOLDEN CAKE MIX OR YELLOW CAKE MIX	1 (520 G)
½ CUP (1 STICK) BUTTER, SOFTENED	125 ML
3 EGGS	3
⅔ CUP ORANGE JUICE	160 ML
1 TEASPOON LEMON ZEST	5 ML
SCANT ¼ CUP POWDERED SUGAR	60 ML

◆ Preheat oven to 350° (176° C). In large bowl, combine cake mix, butter, eggs, orange juice and lemon zest. Beat on low speed to blend, then beat on medium for 2 minutes.

◆ Pour batter into greased, floured 9 x 13-inch (23 x 33 cm) baking dish, and bake for 30 to 35 minutes or until cake tester comes out clean. Remove cake from oven and cool in pan.

◆ When lukewarm, poke holes over surface with toothpick or bamboo skewer and spoon *Lemon Glaze* over top. When glaze soaks into cake, sift powdered sugar lightly over for decoration.

LEMON GLAZE:

⅓ CUP FRESH LEMON JUICE	80 ML
½ CUP HONEY	125 ML

◆ Combine lemon juice and honey in small saucepan. Warm over low heat and stir until they blend.

For lemon zest, see page 10.

DIRT-AND-WORMS CAKE

*This fun dessert is easy to make and the younger
crowd will love it! This is one mud cake you won't
mind them eating! (Also consider this cake for the
gardener in your family and serve it with a plastic toy
trowel. No one is ever too old to have fun with food.)*

1 (18 OUNCE) CHOCOLATE CAKE MIX	1 (520 G)
½ CUP CHOCOLATE SYRUP	125 ML
1 (3 OUNCE) CHOCOLATE FUDGE	
INSTANT PUDDING MIX	1 (85 G)
1¾ CUPS MILK	430 ML
1 CUP CRUSHED CHOCOLATE GRAHAM CRACKERS	
(ABOUT 10) OR OTHER CHOCOLATE COOKIE	250 ML
7 CANDY GUMMI WORMS	7

◆ Preheat oven to 350° (176° C). Prepare cake mix according to package directions for 9 x 13-inch (23 x 33 cm) cake dish and bake. While cake is still hot from oven, poke holes over entire surface using a bamboo skewer. Pour chocolate syrup evenly over cake and cool.

◆ In small bowl, beat pudding mix and milk for 2 minutes, then let it sit for 3 to 5 minutes more until set. Smooth evenly over cake.

◆ Sprinkle crushed graham crackers over pudding. Scatter worms on top, push one end gently into cookie mixture and cover lightly with cookie crumbs, so worms appear to be poking out of the ground. Refrigerate until ready to serve.

Use cake mix with or without pudding.

KEY LIME PIE CAKE

1 (18 OUNCE) WHITE CAKE MIX	**1 (520 G)**
3 EGGS	**3**
2 TABLESPOONS VEGETABLE OIL	**30 ML**
1 TEASPOON LEMON EXTRACT	**5 ML**
1 ⅓ CUPS MILK	**330 ML**
2 CUPS BOILING WATER	**500 ML**
1 (6 OUNCE) PACKAGE LIME GELATIN	**1 (170 G)**

◆ Preheat oven to 350° (176° C). In large bowl, combine cake mix, eggs, oil, lemon extract and milk. Beat on low speed to blend, then beat on medium for 2 minutes.

◆ Pour batter into greased, floured 9 x 13-inch (23 x 33 cm) baking dish. Bake for 30 to 35 minutes or until cake tests done.

◆ Cool cake in pan and poke holes over entire surface using bamboo skewer or long-tined fork.

◆ In medium bowl, stir boiling water into gelatin and stir until gelatin dissolves. Pour over cake and make sure cake is evenly covered.

◆ Refrigerate cake until chills it well and frost with *Marshmallow Icing* on next page.

(CONTINUED ON NEXT PAGE.)

(CONTINUED)

MARSHMALLOW ICING:

2 EGG WHITES	2
⅓ CUP WATER	80 ML
1 ½ CUPS SUGAR	375 ML
¼ TEASPOON CREAM OF TARTAR	1 ML
1 TABLESPOON LIGHT CORN SYRUP	15 ML
2 CUPS MINIATURE MARSHMALLOWS OR	
16 LARGE MARSHMALLOWS, QUARTERED	500 ML
1 TEASPOON CLEAR VANILLA	5 ML

◆ In top of double boiler, combine egg whites, water, sugar, cream of tartar and corn syrup.

◆ Beat with hand mixer until stiff peaks form, about 4 minutes. (Be sure to occasionally scrape bottom and sides of pan.) Remove from heat.

◆ Add marshmallows and vanilla and continue to beat until marshmallows melt and icing reaches spreading consistency (about 2 minutes).

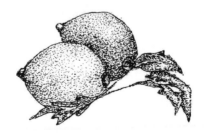

APPLE-CRANBERRY STREUSEL

This moist cake makes a welcome addition to a breakfast gathering or holiday meal. The apple and cranberry flavors are the perfect complement to each other.

1 (18 OUNCE) YELLOW CAKE MIX	1 (520 G)
⅔ CUP APPLE CIDER	160 ML
½ CUP (1 STICK) BUTTER, SOFTENED	125 ML
3 EGGS	3
3 CUPS DICED GRANNY SMITH APPLES	750 ML
¾ CUP DRIED, SWEETENED CRANBERRIES	180 ML
2 TABLESPOONS FLOUR	30 ML
STREUSEL TOPPING	

◆ Preheat oven to 350° (176° C). In large bowl, blend cake mix, cider, butter and eggs on low speed for 30 seconds to blend. Beat at medium speed for 3 minutes.

◆ In medium bowl, combine apples and cranberries with flour and toss to coat. Gently stir into batter until they mix well. Pour batter into greased, floured 9 x 13-inch (23 x 33 cm) baking dish.

◆ Bake for 30 minutes, remove from oven and sprinkle streusel topping evenly over top. Return to oven and bake for another 15 minutes or until cake tester comes out clean.

STREUSEL TOPPING:

1 CUP PACKED LIGHT BROWN SUGAR	250 ML
1 ½ CUPS FLOUR	375 ML
¾ CUP (1 ½ STICKS) BUTTER, SOFTENED	180 ML
½ CUP CHOPPED PECANS	125 ML

◆ In medium bowl, combine all ingredients and mix with fork until they blend well and crumble.

CHERRY STRUDEL

1 (18 OUNCE) WHITE CAKE MIX, DIVIDED	1 (520 G)
1 CUP FLOUR	250 ML
½ CUP SUGAR	125 ML
1 (.25 OUNCE) PACKAGE DRY YEAST	1 (7 G)
⅔ CUP WARM WATER	160 ML
1 TEASPOON BUTTER FLAVORING	5 ML
2 EGGS	2
1 (20 OUNCE) CAN CHERRY PIE FILLING	1 (570 G)
⅓ CUP BUTTER, SOFTENED	80 ML

◆ Preheat oven to 375° (190° C). In large bowl, combine 1½ cups (375 mL) cake mix, flour and sugar. Dissolve yeast in water. Add to dry ingredients in bowl. Stir in butter flavoring and eggs.

◆ Blend thoroughly. Spread batter into greased, floured 9 x 13-inch (23 x 33 cm) baking dish. Spread cherry pie filling over batter.

◆ In small bowl, combine remaining dry cake mix with butter and use fork to blend until crumbly. Sprinkle mixture evenly over pie filling.

◆ Bake for 30 to 35 minutes. Remove from oven, cool and drizzle with glaze.

GLAZE:

1½ CUPS POWDERED SUGAR	375 ML
½ TEASPOON ALMOND EXTRACT	2 ML
3 TABLESPOONS WARM WATER	45 ML

◆ In small bowl, blend sugar, almond extract and water until smooth.

◆ Poke holes in top of cake and drizzle glaze over top.

APPLE-CRUMB CAKE

1 (18 OUNCE) YELLOW CAKE MIX	1 (520 G)
1 (20 OUNCE) CAN APPLE PIE FILLING	1 (570 G)
½ CUP FLOUR	125 ML
½ CUP PACKED BROWN SUGAR	125 ML
½ TEASPOON CINNAMON	2 ML
¼ CUP BUTTER, SOFTENED	60 ML
½ CUP SLIVERED ALMONDS	125 ML

◆ Preheat oven to 350° (176° C). Prepare cake mix according to directions on package, except substitute milk for water (for better consistency).

◆ Pour batter into greased, floured 9 x 13-inch (23 x 33 cm) baking dish. Drop pie filling by spoonfuls evenly over cake batter. (Don't stir.)

◆ In medium bowl, combine flour, brown sugar and cinnamon. Stir until they blend. Cut in butter with fork or pastry cutter until mixture is crumbly.

◆ Stir in almonds. Sprinkle mixture over batter and apples.

◆ Bake for 1 hour or until cake tester comes out clean. Cool and drizzle with *Powdered Sugar Icing*.

POWDERED SUGAR ICING:

4 TEASPOONS WARM WATER	20 ML
1 CUP POWDERED SUGAR	250 ML

◆ In small bowl, stir water into powdered sugar until mixture is smooth and spread over top of cake.

CHERRY-ALMOND STRUDEL

1 (18 OUNCE) LEMON CAKE MIX WITH PUDDING	1 (520 G)
¼ CUP (½ STICK) BUTTER, SOFTENED	60 ML
1 (3 OUNCE) PACKAGE CREAM CHEESE, SOFTENED	1 (85 G)
⅓ CUP WATER	80 ML
½ TEASPOON ALMOND EXTRACT	2 ML
2 EGGS	2
1 (20 OUNCE) CAN CHERRY PIE FILLING	1 (520 G)
½ CUP CHOPPED ALMONDS	125 ML

◆ Preheat oven to 350° (176° C). In large bowl, combine cake mix, butter and cream cheese. Beat at low speed until crumbly. Reserve 1 cup crumb mixture for topping and set aside.

◆ Add water, almond extract and eggs to remaining crumb mixture and beat on high speed for 2 minutes. (The batter will become very smooth and fluffy.) Spread in greased, floured 9 x 13-inch (23 x 33 cm) baking dish.

◆ Gently spread cherry pie filling over batter and smooth carefully to distribute evenly.

◆ Mix almonds with reserved crumb mixture and sprinkle over pie filling.

◆ Bake for 35 minutes or until cake tester inserted in center comes out clean and edges are light brown. Remove from oven and cool for about 30 minutes. Drizzle glaze over warm cake.

GLAZE:

½ CUP POWDERED SUGAR	125 ML
1 TABLESPOON BUTTER, SOFTENED	15 ML
2 TO 3 TEASPOONS MILK OR CREAM	10 TO 15 ML
¼ TEASPOON ALMOND EXTRACT	1 ML

◆ In small bowl, combine sugar, butter, milk and almond extract. Blend well.

◆ Poke holes in top of cake and drizzle glaze.

RICOTTA-RAISIN CAKE

Because the cheese and raisins form a layer beneath the cake as it bakes, I like to serve the slices upside-down, so that the raisins dot the top of the cake and the cheese layer forms a kind of topping. For especially good flavor, serve the cake warm.

1 (18 OUNCE) LEMON CAKE MIX	1 (520 G)
1 (15 OUNCE) CONTAINER RICOTTA CHEESE	1 (438 G)
4 EGGS	4
1 CUP SUGAR	250 ML
1 TEASPOON CINNAMON	5 ML
1 TEASPOON VANILLA	5 ML
1 CUP RAISINS	250 ML
1 TABLESPOON ORANGE ZEST	15 ML

◆ Preheat oven to 325° (163° C). Prepare cake mix according to package directions, except substitute milk for water. Pour batter into greased, floured 9 x 13-inch (23 x 33 cm) baking pan.

◆ In large bowl, combine cheese, eggs, sugar, cinnamon and vanilla. Beat on low speed for 1 to 2 minutes to blend. Stir in raisins and orange zest.

◆ Spoon mixture evenly over cake batter. Bake for 1 hour or until cake tester comes out clean. Cool slightly and serve with *Rum Sauce* (next page) on top.

(CONTINUED ON NEXT PAGE.)

For Orange Zest, see page 10.

(CONTINUED)

RUM SAUCE:

⅓ CUP BUTTER	**80 ML**
⅔ CUP SUGAR	**160 ML**
⅓ CUP HALF-AND-HALF	**80 ML**
2 TABLESPOONS RUM	**30 ML**
1 TEASPOON VANILLA	**5 ML**

◆ Combine butter, sugar and half-and-half in medium saucepan. Cook over medium heat, stirring constantly, until butter melts and mixture is slightly thick (about 5 minutes).

◆ Stir in rum and vanilla and cook for a few minutes more. Cool slightly and serve over cake.

LEMON CAKE

This cake is very moist with a tangy lemon flavor. The topping finishes it off with very little effort and really enhances the flavor of the cake. It's sweet, but not overly rich.

1 (18 OUNCE) LEMON CAKE MIX	**1 (520 G)**
1 (20 OUNCE) CAN CRUSHED PINEAPPLE	
WITH JUICE	**1 (570 G)**
3 EGGS	**3**
⅓ CUP VEGETABLE OIL	**80 ML**

◆ Preheat oven to 350° (176° C). In large bowl, combine cake mix, pineapple with juice, eggs and oil. Blend on low speed to moisten, then beat on medium for 2 minutes.

◆ Pour batter into greased, floured 9 x 13-inch (23 x 33 cm) baking dish. Bake for 30 minutes. Remove from oven and spread topping evenly over top.

◆ Return cake to oven and bake for additional 10 minutes. Cool and keep refrigerated.

TOPPING:

1 (14 OUNCE) CAN SWEETENED CONDENSED MILK	**1 (420 G)**
1 CUP SOUR CREAM	**250 ML**
¼ CUP FRESH LEMON JUICE	**60 ML**

◆ In medium bowl, combine sweetened condensed milk, sour cream and lemon juice. Stir well to blend and spread over top.

EARTHQUAKE CAKE

An outrageously delicious cake — you'll be hooked after your first bite. It makes a great "1-step" cake because it needs no frosting. If you have any doubts, try it.

1 CUP SHREDDED COCONUT	250 ML
1 CUP CHOPPED PECANS	250 ML
½ CUP WHITE CHOCOLATE CHIPS	125 ML
1 (18 OUNCE) DEVIL'S FOOD CAKE MIX	1 (520 G)
1 (8 OUNCE) PACKAGE CREAM CHEESE, SOFTENED	1 (228 G)
½ CUP (1 STICK) BUTTER	125 ML
1 (1 POUND) BOX POWDERED SUGAR	1 (454 G)
1 TEASPOON VANILLA	5 ML

◆ Preheat oven to 350° (176° C). Sprinkle coconut, pecans and white chocolate chips evenly in bottom of a lightly greased 9 x 13-inch (23 x 33 cm) baking dish.

◆ Mix cake according to package directions and pour over mixture in pan.

◆ In medium bowl, thoroughly blend cream cheese, butter, powdered sugar and vanilla.

◆ Drop by spoonfuls onto cake mixture, covering entire surface, but do not stir. Bake for 40 to 45 minutes.

APRICOT-RASPBERRY UPSIDE-DOWN CAKE

6 TABLESPOONS BUTTER, MELTED	**90 ML**
1 CUP PACKED LIGHT BROWN SUGAR	**250 ML**
1 (21 OUNCE) CAN APRICOTS IN HEAVY SYRUP	**1 (598 G)**
1 CUP FROZEN RASPBERRIES	**250 ML**
1 (18 OUNCE) WHITE CAKE MIX	**1 (520 G)**
3 TABLESPOONS VEGETABLE OIL	**45 ML**
⅓ CUP MILK	**80 ML**
3 EGGS	**3**

◆ Preheat oven to 350° (176° C). Pour melted butter in 9 x 13-inch (23 x 33 cm) baking dish. Sprinkle brown sugar evenly over butter.

◆ Slice apricots and save ¾ cup (180 mL) syrup. Place apricot slices evenly over brown sugar and arrange raspberries around apricots. Set aside.

◆ In large bowl, combine cake mix, reserved ¾ cup (180 mL) apricot syrup, oil, milk and eggs. Beat on low speed to blend, then beat on medium for about 2 minutes.

◆ Pour batter carefully over apricots and raspberries and cover evenly. Bake for 30 to 35 minutes or until cake tester comes out clean.

◆ Immediately upon removing from oven, turn cake out of pan onto cookie sheet or cake board. Let pan rest upside-down for 1 minute before removing it to allow all of topping to drip onto cake. Cool cake and serve warm or cold. Refrigerate to keep fresh.

PINEAPPLE UPSIDE-DOWN CAKE

This classic couldn't be easier—it ices itself!
Also, for a more robust citrus flavor, substitute
lemon cake mix for the white.

6 TABLESPOONS BUTTER	**90 ML**
1 (20 OUNCE) CAN PINEAPPLE, SLICED OR	
CRUSHED WITH JUICE	**1 (570 G)**
½ CUP CHOPPED PECANS	**125 ML**
1 ⅓ CUPS PACKED LIGHT BROWN SUGAR	**330 ML**
1 (18 OUNCE) WHITE CAKE MIX	**1 (520 G)**

◆ Preheat oven to 350° (176° C). Melt butter in 9 x 13-inch (23 x 33 cm) baking dish. Drain pineapple and reserve ¾ cup (180 mL) juice.

◆ Sprinkle nuts in bottom of dish and cover evenly with brown sugar. Arrange pineapple slices or crushed pineapple on top.

◆ Prepare cake mix according to package directions, except replace ¾ cup (180 mL) liquid with reserved pineapple juice.

◆ Pour over brown sugar and bake for 45 to 50 minutes or until cake top springs back when touched.

SELF-FROSTING
MEXICAN CHOCOLATE CAKE

*What a fun and easy cake. The marshmallow
mixture cooks to a pudding-like consistency
with an intense chocolate flavor. (This cake will
appeal to those who prefer less rich frostings.)*

2 ½ CUPS MINI-MARSHMALLOWS	**625 ML**
1 CUP PACKED BROWN SUGAR	**250 ML**
½ CUP COCOA POWDER	**125 ML**
2 CUPS HOT WATER	**500 ML**
1 (18 OUNCE) DEVIL'S FOOD CAKE MIX	**1 (520 G)**
1 ⅓ CUPS BUTTERMILK	**330 ML**
3 EGGS	**3**
⅓ CUP VEGETABLE OIL	**80 ML**
2 TEASPOONS CINNAMON	**10 ML**
1 TEASPOON VANILLA	**5 ML**
1 (1 OUNCE) SQUARE UNSWEETENED	
CHOCOLATE, MELTED	**1 (28 G)**
½ CUP CHOPPED PECANS, TOASTED	**125 ML**

◆ Preheat oven to 350° (176° C). Sprinkle marshmallows evenly in bottom of greased, floured 9 x 13-inch (23 x 33 cm) baking dish. In medium bowl, mix sugar, cocoa and hot water. Pour over marshmallows.

◆ In large bowl, combine cake mix, buttermilk, eggs, oil, cinnamon, vanilla and melted chocolate. Beat on low speed to blend, then beat on medium for 3 minutes. Pour batter evenly over marshmallow mixture.

◆ Bake for 45 minutes or until cake tester inserted into top half of cake comes out clean. Remove pan from oven and cool for 20 to 30 minutes. Turn cake out of pan onto serving tray. Use butter knife or spatula to smooth frosting on sides and top of cake. Sprinkle pecans evenly over top.

CHERRY COLA CAKE

What could be better than a chocolate cake loaded with cherry flavor and topped with sweet cherries? This easy cake is another good standby when you need a quick, delicious cake with little fuss or effort. When you turn it out of the pan, it's ready to go with the cherries on top to form an attractive and tasteful "icing". Since you don't have to worry about frosting getting messed up while you're carrying it, this is a great cake to take to get-togethers.

2 (15 OUNCE) CANS DARK SWEET CHERRIES	
WITH SYRUP	**2 (438 G)**
2 (3 OUNCE) PACKAGES CHERRY GELATIN,	
DIVIDED	**2 (85 G)**
1 CUP COLA, DIVIDED	**250 ML**
⅛ TEASPOON ALMOND EXTRACT	**.5 ML**
2 CUPS MINIATURE-MARSHMALLOWS	**500 ML**
1 (18 OUNCE) GERMAN CHOCOLATE CAKE MIX	**1 (520 G)**
½ CUP VEGETABLE OIL	**125 ML**
4 EGGS	**4**

◆ Preheat oven to 350° (176° C). Remove cherry pits and save ¾ cup (180 mL) syrup. Arrange cherries in bottom of greased, floured 9 x 13-inch (23 x 33 cm) baking dish.

◆ In small saucepan, combine cherry syrup, 1 package gelatin and ¼ cup (60 mL) cola. Stir over low heat until gelatin dissolves. Add almond extract and remove from heat to cool slightly.

◆ Pour over cherries and sprinkle evenly with marshmallows.

◆ In large bowl, combine cake mix, remaining package gelatin, oil, eggs and remaining cola. Beat on high speed for 3 minutes.

◆ Carefully spread batter over marshmallows. Bake for 40 to 45 minutes or until cake tester comes out clean.

◆ Remove from oven and cool for about 45 minutes. Turn out of pan onto serving plate. Chill before serving and keep refrigerated.

RASPBERRY RUM-RAISIN CAKE

¾ CUP RAISINS	180 ML
¾ CUP LIGHT RUM	180 ML
3 EGGS	3
½ CUP WATER	125 ML
¼ CUP VEGETABLE OIL	60 ML
1 (3 OUNCE) PACKAGE RASPBERRY GELATIN	1 (85 G)
1 (18 OUNCE) BOX WHITE CAKE MIX	1 (520 G)

◆ Cover raisins with rum and soak for several hours to plump them up, drain and reserve rum.

◆ Preheat oven to 350° (176° C).

◆ In medium bowl, beat eggs until foamy, about 2 minutes. Add water, oil and reserved rum and beat on medium speed. While continuing to beat, slowly add raspberry gelatin and cake mix, a little at a time, until fully incorporated. Beat for 2 minutes.

◆ Gently stir raisins into batter and pour batter into greased, floured, 12-cup (3 L) bundt cake pan. Bake for 45 minutes or until cake tester comes out clean. Cool for 15 minutes and then turn cake out of pan.

◆ Cool and frost with *Rum Glaze*.

RUM GLAZE:

1 CUP (2 STICKS) BUTTER	250 ML
¼ CUP WATER	60 ML
1 CUP SUGAR	250 ML
½ CUP RUM	125 ML

◆ In medium saucepan, bring butter, water and sugar to boil. Boil for 5 minutes, stirring constantly. Remove from heat and stir in rum. Spoon over cake.

You don't have to soak the raisins if you're short on time, just add them right out of the package.

PINEAPPLE-RUM CAKE

1 (18 OUNCE) YELLOW CAKE MIX	**1 (520 G)**
1 (3 OUNCE) PACKAGE VANILLA INSTANT PUDDING	**1 (85 G)**
1 (8 OUNCE) CAN CRUSHED PINEAPPLE WITH JUICE	**1 (228 G)**
4 EGGS	**4**
½ CUP RUM	**125 ML**
⅓ CUP VEGETABLE OIL	**60 ML**

◆ Preheat oven to 350° (176° C). In large bowl, combine cake mix, pudding mix, pineapple with juice, eggs, rum and oil. Beat on low speed to blend, then beat on medium for 2 minutes.

◆ Pour batter into greased, floured, 12-cup (3 L) bundt cake pan and bake for 50 to 55 minutes or until cake tester comes out clean.

◆ Cool in pan for 10 minutes, then turn out onto serving platter. Poke holes about ½ inch apart over surface of cake using bamboo skewer or long-tined fork. Spoon *Butter Rum Glaze* over top.

BUTTER-RUM GLAZE:

½ CUP BUTTER	**125 ML**
¼ CUP WATER	**60 ML**
1 CUP SUGAR	**250 ML**
½ CUP RUM	**125 ML**

◆ In medium saucepan, melt butter over low heat. Add water and sugar and stir to blend thoroughly. Boil for 5 minutes.

◆ Remove from heat and stir in rum. Cool slightly and spoon over cake. Recover glaze that pools around bottom of cake and spoon over top again so cake absorbs as much as possible.

You may use margarine instead of butter for the glaze, but it really won't taste as good. Since this is the finishing touch on the cake, you want to make it taste as good as it can.

PUMPKIN-RUM CAKE

*This dense cake is very moist and keeps really well.
There's just enough rum in the mix to give a hint
of rum flavor to the cake, which goes well with the
pumpkin. And its vibrant orange color will add a
festive look to any table, especially at Thanksgiving.*

1 (18 OUNCE) WHITE CAKE MIX	1 (520 G)
1 (15 OUNCE) CAN PUMPKIN	1 (438 G)
3 EGGS	3
½ CUP RUM	125 ML
¾ CUP CHOPPED PECANS, TOASTED	180 ML

◆ Preheat oven to 325° (163° C). In large bowl, combine cake mix, pumpkin, eggs and rum. Beat on low speed to blend, then beat on medium for 2 minutes. Stir in pecans until they blend well.

◆ Pour batter into greased, floured, 12-cup (3 L) bundt cake pan. Bake for 45 to 50 minutes or until cake tester comes out clean.

◆ Let cake cool in pan for 10 minutes, then turn out onto serving platter and frost with *Orange Glaze*.

ORANGE GLAZE:

1 CUP POWDERED SUGAR	250 ML
2 TABLESPOONS PLUS	30 ML +
½ TEASPOON ORANGE JUICE	2 ML
1 TABLESPOON ORANGE ZEST	15 ML

◆ Mix powdered sugar, orange juice and orange zest until smooth. Spoon over top of cake and let icing run down the sides.

To toast pecans and for orange zest, see page 10.

SPICY WALNUT-RUM CAKE

1 (18 OUNCE) SPICE CAKE MIX	1 (520 G)
4 EGGS	4
1 ⅓ CUPS BUTTERMILK	330 ML
⅓ CUP VEGETABLE OIL	80 ML
½ CUP PACKED BROWN SUGAR	125 ML
1 ½ CUPS CHOPPED WALNUTS, TOASTED	375 ML

◆ Preheat oven to 325° (163° C). In large bowl, combine cake mix, eggs, buttermilk, oil and brown sugar. Beat on low speed to blend, then beat on medium for 2 minutes. Stir in walnuts until they blend well.

◆ Pour batter into greased, floured, 12-cup (3 L) bundt cake pan. Bake for 50 to 55 minutes or until cake tester comes out clean.

◆ Remove from oven and cool in pan for 10 minutes. Leave in pan and poke holes over entire surface of cake bottom using a bamboo skewer or a long tined-fork. Use large spoon to pour *Rum Syrup* evenly over top and let it soak in after each spoonful. Let cake remain in pan until fully cool, about 2 hours, then turn out onto serving platter.

RUM SYRUP:

1 CUP RUM	250 ML
1 CUP SUGAR	250 ML
¼ CUP (½ STICK) BUTTER	60 ML

◆ Combine rum, sugar and butter in medium saucepan. Bring to simmer, stirring frequently, and cook for 2 minutes. Remove from heat and spoon over cake.

You can use margarine for the Rum Syrup, but it doesn't taste as good as butter. I always use butter when I make this.

To make buttermilk from milk, see page 10.

COCONUT-FILLED
CHOCOLATE CAKE

*The white coconut running through the center of
this cake looks pretty against the dark chocolate.*

1 (18 OUNCE) DEVIL'S FOOD CAKE MIX	**1 (520 G)**
1 EGG WHITE	**1**
¼ CUP SUGAR	**60 ML**
1 CUP SHREDDED COCONUT	**250 ML**
1 TABLESPOON FLOUR	**15 ML**
1 TEASPOON CLEAR VANILLA	**5 ML**

◆ Preheat oven to 350° (163° C). Prepare cake mix according to package directions except use buttermilk instead of water to make it richer.

◆ In medium bowl, beat egg white until soft peaks form. Gradually add sugar and continue to beat until stiff peaks form.

◆ Fold in coconut, flour and vanilla.

◆ Pour half prepared cake mix batter into greased, floured, 12-cup (3 L) bundt cake pan.

◆ Drop coconut filling by spoonfuls evenly over center of batter in pan, but avoid touching the sides.

◆ Pour remaining batter over top and smooth.

(CONTINUED ON NEXT PAGE.)

To make buttermilk, see page 10.

54

(CONTINUED)

◆ Bake for 45 minutes or until cake tester comes out clean.

◆ Cool cake in pan for 10 minutes, then turn out onto cooling rack. When cool, ice with *Milk Chocolate Glaze*.

MILK CHOCOLATE GLAZE:
⅓ CUP EVAPORATED MILK	80 ML
¾ CUP MILK CHOCOLATE CHIPS	180 ML

◆ In medium saucepan, melt chocolate chips in milk over medium heat. (Mixture will be thin.)

◆ Cool to lukewarm and spoon over cake, covering entire surface.

If you're using shortening and flour to grease the pan, use cocoa powder in place of flour to give a nice even color on cake's surface when it comes out of the pan.

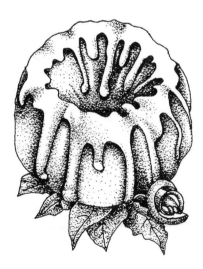

ORANGE BUNDT CAKE
WITH CITRUS-RUM SAUCE

1 (18 OUNCE) BUTTER RECIPE GOLDEN CAKE MIX	1 (520 G)
3 EGGS	3
⅔ CUP ORANGE JUICE	160 ML
½ CUP (1 STICK) BUTTER, SOFTENED	125 ML
4 TABLESPOONS ORANGE ZEST	60 ML

◆ Preheat oven to 350° (176° C). In large bowl, combine cake mix, eggs, orange juice, butter and orange zest. Beat on low speed to blend, then beat on medium for 3 minutes.

◆ Pour batter into greased, floured 12-cup (3 L) bundt cake pan and bake for 45 to 50 minutes or until cake tester comes out clean.

◆ Cool cake slightly in pan. With cake in pan, poke holes ½ inch apart over entire surface of cake with bamboo skewer or long-tined fork.

◆ Spoon *Citrus Rum Sauce* below, evenly over top and let it soak into cake. Leave cake in pan for another 2 hours to absorb sauce, turn out onto serving plate and dust with powdered sugar.

CITRUS RUM SAUCE:

½ CUP SUGAR	125 ML
¼ CUP WATER	60 ML
¼ CUP ORANGE JUICE	60 ML
2 TABLESPOONS LEMON JUICE	30 ML
2 TABLESPOONS RUM	30 ML

◆ Combine sugar and water in medium saucepan and bring to a boil. Boil for 1 minute, stirring frequently, and remove from heat. Cool slightly. Stir in orange juice, lemon juice and rum.

For orange zest, see page 10.

APRICOT-BRANDY CAKE

1 (18 OUNCE) YELLOW CAKE MIX	**1 (520 G)**
1 (3 OUNCE) LEMON PUDDING MIX	**1 (85 G)**
4 EGGS	**4**
1 CUP SOUR CREAM	**250 ML**
½ CUP BRANDY	**125 ML**
1 (15 OUNCE) CAN APRICOT HALVES, SLICED	**1 (438 G)**

◆ Preheat oven to 350° (176° C). In large bowl, combine cake mix, pudding mix, eggs, sour cream and brandy.

◆ Beat on low speed to blend, then beat on medium for 2 minutes more. Gently fold in apricot slices.

◆ Pour batter into greased, floured, 12-cup (3 L) bundt cake pan. Bake for 50 to 55 minutes or until cake tester comes out clean.

◆ Cool in pan for 10 minutes, then turn out onto serving platter. When cool, sprinkle with powdered sugar.

ANISETTE-EASTER CAKE

*This cake is a version of an Italian Easter cake that my
mother makes from a recipe handed down from her
father, who came to the U.S. from Rome. The original cake
has a more bread-like texture and is very dense and less
sweet. It's a family tradition to eat the cakes on Easter
morning with butter and capicola, a cured Italian ham.
This dessert version is much quicker to make than the original.
For one thing you don't have to let the cakes rise!*

1 (18 OUNCE) WHITE CAKE MIX	1 (520 G)
1 (3 OUNCE) VANILLA INSTANT PUDDING MIX	1 (85 G)
¼ CUP SUGAR	60 ML
3 EGGS	3
⅓ CUP HALF-AND-HALF	80 ML
⅓ CUP VEGETABLE OIL	80 ML
⅔ CUP ANISETTE	160 ML
3 TABLESPOONS ANISE SEEDS*	45 ML
2 TABLESPOONS LEMON JUICE	30 ML
1 TABLESPOON LEMON ZEST	15 ML

◆ Preheat oven to 350º (176º C). In large bowl, combine cake
mix, pudding mix, sugar, eggs, half-and-half, oil, anisette mixture,
lemon juice and zest.

◆ Beat on low speed to blend, then beat on medium for 2 minutes.
Pour batter into greased, floured, 12-cup (3 L) bundt pan.

◆ Bake for 50 minutes or until cake tester comes out clean. Cool
for 10 minutes in pan and turn out onto cooling rack.

◆ When cool, ice with *Butter Lemon Icing* on next page.

(CONTINUED ON NEXT PAGE.)

(CONTINUED)

BUTTER LEMON ICING:

3 TABLESPOONS BUTTER, SOFTENED	45 ML
1 CUP POWDERED SUGAR	250 ML
1 TABLESPOON LEMON ZEST	15 ML
3 TEASPOONS HALF-AND-HALF	15 ML

◆ In medium bowl, cream butter with sugar until smooth. Add lemon zest and blend. Add-half-and half 1 teaspoon (5 mL) at a time and blend well after each addition.

◆ This recipe makes enough icing to frost the crown of the cake. You can double the recipe if you want to frost the entire cake.

* Soak the anise seeds in anisette overnight or longer to soften them. I usually put them in a small container with a tight-fitting lid. Add the anise seeds to the anisette, stir to mix and cover. You can soak the seeds for several days, if you want.

For lemon zest, see page 10.

AMARETTO CAKE

1 (18 OUNCE) WHITE CAKE MIX	1 (520 G)
1 (3 OUNCE) VANILLA INSTANT PUDDING MIX	1 (85 G)
4 EGGS	4
2 TABLESPOONS AMARETTO LIQUEUR	30 ML
½ CUP WATER	125 ML
½ CUP VEGETABLE OIL	125 ML
½ CUP SLICED ALMONDS	125 ML

◆ Preheat oven to 350° (176° C). In large bowl, combine cake mix, pudding mix, eggs, amaretto, water and oil.

◆ Beat on low speed to blend, then beat on medium speed for 2 minutes.

◆ Sprinkle almonds into bottom of greased, floured 12-cup (3 L) bundt cake pan. Pour batter over almonds.

◆ Bake for 40 to 45 minutes or until cake tester comes out clean. Remove from oven, poke holes over bottom of cake with bamboo skewer or long-tined fork, pour *Amaretto Icing* evenly over top and let it soak into holes.

◆ Leave cake in pan for at least 2 hours before removing to give icing a chance to soak into cake.

AMARETTO ICING:

½ CUP AMARETTO LIQUEUR	125 ML
1 CUP POWDERED SUGAR	250 ML

◆ In medium bowl, combine amaretto with sugar and blend until mixture is smooth and pour over cake.

LEMON-BLUEBERRY BUNDT CAKE WITH HONEY-LEMON GLAZE

1 (18 OUNCE) LEMON CAKE MIX	1 (520 G)
1 (3 OUNCE) VANILLA INSTANT PUDDING MIX	1 (85 G)
1 (8 OUNCE) CONTAINER VANILLA YOGURT	1 (228 G)
3 EGGS	3
⅓ CUP OIL	80 ML
2 CUPS FRESH OR FROZEN BLUEBERRIES	500 ML
2 TABLESPOONS FLOUR	30 ML

◆ Preheat oven to 350⁰ (176° C). In large bowl, combine cake mix, pudding mix, yogurt, eggs and oil. Beat on low speed to blend, then beat on medium for 2 minutes.

◆ In small bowl, toss blueberries gently with flour to coat. Stir carefully into batter.

◆ Pour batter into greased, floured, 12-cup (3 L) bundt cake pan. Bake for 50 to 55 minutes or until cake tester comes out clean. Cool cake in pan for 10 minutes, then turn out onto serving platter. Cool and spoon *Honey Lemon Glaze* over top.

HONEY LEMON GLAZE:

2 TABLESPOONS SUGAR	30 ML
¼ CUP HONEY	60 ML
1 TABLESPOON LEMON JUICE	15 ML
1 TABLESPOON BUTTER	15 ML

◆ In small saucepan, bring sugar, honey, lemon juice and butter to boil, stirring constantly. Boil gently for 1 minute and remove from heat. Cool for several minutes, then spoon over cake.

After spooning glaze over cake, I generally scoop up some of the glaze pooled around bottom of cake and spoon it over the cake again to cover places that were missed the first time. Not only does this cover the cake better, but it also gives the glaze a chance to soak into the cake a little bit.

61

APRICOT-STREUSEL BUNDT CAKE

1 (18 OUNCE) YELLOW CAKE MIX	1 (520 G)
1 (3 OUNCE) VANILLA INSTANT PUDDING MIX	1 (85 G)
1 (15 OUNCE) CAN APRICOT HALVES	
WITH HEAVY SYRUP	1 (438 G)
4 EGGS	4
½ CUP VEGETABLE OIL	125 ML
½ CUP PACKED BROWN SUGAR	125 ML
2 TEASPOONS CINNAMON	10 ML
½ CUP FINELY CHOPPED PECANS	125 ML

◆ Preheat oven to 350° (176° C). Drain 1 cup (250 mL) syrup from apricots and set aside; slice apricots. In large bowl, combine cake mix, pudding mix, apricot syrup, eggs and oil.

◆ Beat on low speed to blend, then beat on medium for 2 minutes.

◆ In small bowl, combine sugar, cinnamon and pecans and mix well.

◆ Pour half batter into greased, floured, 12-cup (3 L) bundt cake pan. Place half sliced apricots evenly over batter and sprinkle half sugar mixture over top.

◆ Gently pour remaining batter on top and smooth over top. Layer other half of apricots and sprinkle with remaining sugar mixture.

◆ Bake for 55 to 60 minutes or until cake tester comes out clean. Cool in pan for 10 minutes, then turn out onto cooling rack. Ice with *Powdered Sugar Glaze* on next page.

(CONTINUED ON NEXT PAGE.)

(CONTINUED)

POWDERED SUGAR GLAZE:

¾ CUP POWDERED SUGAR	180 ML
½ TEASPOON CLEAR VANILLA	2 ML
3 TEASPOONS WARM WATER	15 ML

◆ In small bowl, mix sugar, vanilla and water. If needed, add water a couple of drops at a time as needed until icing reaches drizzling consistency.

◆ Drizzle over cake, use knife to spread more evenly on top of cake and let it run down sides. (Note: You need to work fast with this glaze, because it hardens quickly.)

BLUEBERRY CREAM CHEESE CAKE

1 (18 OUNCE) YELLOW CAKE MIX	1 (520 G)
4 EGGS	4
½ CUP MILK	125 ML
¼ CUP VEGETABLE OIL	60 ML
½ CUP SUGAR	125 ML
1 TEASPOON ALMOND EXTRACT	5 ML
1 (8 OUNCE) PACKAGE CREAM CHEESE, SOFTENED	1 (228 G)
1 ½ CUPS FRESH OR FROZEN BLUEBERRIES	375 ML
1 TABLESPOON FLOUR	15 ML
POWDERED SUGAR	

◆ Preheat oven to 350⁰ (176⁰ C). In large bowl, combine cake mix, eggs, milk, oil, sugar and almond extract. Beat on low speed to blend. Add cream cheese and beat on medium for 2 minutes. In small bowl, toss blueberries with flour to coat. Gently stir into batter.

◆ Pour batter into greased, floured, 12-cup (3 L) bundt cake pan and bake for 50 to 55 minutes or until cake tester comes out clean. Cool in pan for 10 minutes, then turn out onto serving platter. Dust with powdered sugar, if desired.

ORANGE-TOPPED
LEMON BUNDT CAKE

1 (18 OUNCE) JAR ORANGE MARMALADE	**1 (520 G)**
⅔ CUP SHREDDED COCONUT	**160 ML**
6 TABLESPOONS (¾ STICK) BUTTER, MELTED	**90 ML**
1 (18 OUNCE) YELLOW CAKE MIX	**1 (520 G)**
1 (3 OUNCE) LEMON INSTANT PUDDING MIX	**1 (85 G)**
4 EGGS	**4**
1 CUP ORANGE JUICE	**250 ML**
⅓ CUP VEGETABLE OIL	**80 ML**

◆ Preheat oven to 350° (176° C). In small bowl, combine orange marmalade, coconut and butter. Mix well.

◆ Pour mixture into bottom of greased, floured, 12-cup (3 L) bundt cake pan.

◆ In large bowl, combine cake mix, pudding mix, eggs, orange juice and oil. Beat on low speed to blend, then beat on medium speed for 2 minutes.

◆ Pour batter over orange mixture in pan. Bake for 50 to 60 minutes or until cake tests done.

◆ Cool in pan for 10 minutes, then turn out onto serving plate.

You may substitute the orange marmalade with pineapple preserves for a nice change. They have a sharper citrus flavor that goes really well with the flavors of lemon and orange in the cake.

WHITE CHOCOLATE BUNDT CAKE

2 CUPS WHITE CHOCOLATE CHIPS, DIVIDED	**500 ML**
1 CUP MILK	**250 ML**
1 (18 OUNCE) WHITE CAKE MIX	**1 (520 G)**
1 (3 OUNCE) WHITE CHOCOLATE	
OR VANILLA INSTANT PUDDING MIX	**1 (85 G)**
4 EGGS	**4**
⅓ CUP VEGETABLE OIL	**80 ML**
1 TABLESPOON FLOUR	**15 ML**

◆ Preheat oven to 350° (176° C). In small saucepan, combine 1 cup (250 mL) baking chips with milk and melt over low heat, stirring constantly, until mixture is smooth. Cool.

◆ In large bowl, combine cake mix, pudding mix, chocolate mixture, eggs and oil. Beat on low speed to moisten and on medium speed for 2 minutes, until it blends well.

◆ Coat remaining baking chips with flour and stir into batter. Pour batter into greased, floured, 12-cup (3 L) bundt cake pan and bake for 50 minutes or until cake tester comes out clean. Frost.

WHITE CHOCOLATE ICING:

¾ CUP WHITE CHOCOLATE BAKING CHIPS	**180 ML**
1 TABLESPOON FLOUR	**15 ML**
½ CUP MILK	**125 ML**
½ CUP (1 STICK) BUTTER	**125 ML**
1 CUP POWDERED SUGAR	**250 ML**
1 TEASPOON VANILLA	**5 ML**

◆ In small saucepan, combine baking chips, flour and milk. Cook over medium heat, stirring constantly, until chocolate melts completely and mixture thickens (about 3 minutes). Remove from heat and cool.

◆ In medium bowl, combine butter, powdered sugar and vanilla and beat until light and fluffy, about 2 minutes. Slowly add white chocolate mixture and beat until it blends well.

NEVER-ENDING
CHOCOLATE BUNDT CAKE

1 (18 OUNCE) DEVIL'S FOOD CAKE MIX	1 (520 G)
1 (3 OUNCE) DARK FUDGE INSTANT PUDDING MIX	1 (85 G)
1 ¼ CUPS BUTTERMILK	310 ML
½ CUP VEGETABLE OIL	125 ML
½ CUP CHOCOLATE SYRUP	125 ML
4 EGGS	4
1 CUP SEMI-SWEET CHOCOLATE CHIPS	250 ML

◆ Preheat oven to 325° (163° C). In large bowl, combine cake mix, pudding mix, milk, oil, syrup and eggs.

◆ Beat on low speed to blend, then beat on medium speed for 2 to 3 minutes.

◆ Gently stir in chocolate chips and pour batter into greased, floured, 12-cup (3 L) bundt cake pan.

◆ Bake for 55 minutes to 1 hour or until cake tester comes out clean. Cool cake in pan for 10 minutes and turn out onto cooling rack.

◆ Sprinkle with powdered sugar for garnish or drizzle with *Chocolate Glaze* on next page.

(CONTINUED ON NEXT PAGE.)

(CONTINUED)

CHOCOLATE GLAZE:

1 CUP SEMI-SWEET CHOCOLATE CHIPS	250 ML
⅔ CUP EVAPORATED MILK	160 ML

◆ Combine chocolate and milk in small saucepan. Cook and stir over low heat until they blend and mixture comes to a boil.

◆ Lower heat and cook, stirring constantly until it thickens.

WHITE CHOCOLATE DRIZZLING GLAZE:
¼ CUP WHITE CHOCOLATE BAKING CHIPS, MELTED 60 ML

◆ For a quick and easy way to drizzle glaze, put melted chocolate in plastic bag (like a sandwich bag) and snip off a corner. Squeeze bag gently to drizzle chocolate.

To make it look extra special, drizzle White Chocolate Glaze on over the dark chocolate glaze. It adds a lot of pizzazz for a professional-looking touch.

CHERRY CORDIAL CAKE

3 EGGS	3
¼ CUP WATER	60 ML
½ CUP VEGETABLE OIL	125 ML
1 (18 OUNCE) WHITE CAKE MIX	1 (520 G)
1 (3 OUNCE) PACKAGE CHERRY INSTANT GELATIN	1 (85 G)
1 (16 OUNCE) JAR MARASCHINO CHERRIES	
WITH JUICE	1 (454 G)

◆ Preheat oven to 350° (176° C). Beat eggs on high speed until foamy, about 2 minutes. Blend water and oil with eggs.

◆ Slowly add cake mix and gelatin, beating constantly. Add ¾ cup (180 mL) maraschino cherry juice and beat for 2 minutes more.

◆ Coarsely chop cherries and gently stir into batter.

◆ Pour batter into greased, floured, 12-cup (3 L) bundt cake pan and bake for approximately 45 minutes or until cake tester comes out clean. When cool, ice with *Chocolate Glaze*.

CHOCOLATE GLAZE:

6 (1 OUNCE) SQUARES	
SEMI-SWEET BAKING CHOCOLATE	6 (28 G)
⅔ CUP EVAPORATED MILK	160 ML

◆ In small saucepan, combine chocolate and evaporated milk. Cook and stir over low heat until mixture comes to a boil.

◆ Lower heat and cook gently for 3 to 5 minutes, stirring constantly until it thickens. Cool, stirring occasionally and drizzle over top.

DATE-SPICE CAKE
WITH BROWN SUGAR GLAZE

1 (18 OUNCE) SPICE CAKE MIX	1 (520 G)
4 EGGS	4
1 CUP SOUR CREAM	250 G
⅓ CUP VEGETABLE OIL	80 G
½ CUP MOLASSES	125 ML
¾ CUP CHOPPED DATES	180 ML
¾ CUP CHOPPED WALNUTS	180 ML

◆ Preheat oven to 325° (163° C). In large bowl, combine cake mix, eggs, sour cream, oil and molasses. Beat on low speed to blend, then beat on medium speed for 2 minutes.

◆ Stir in dates and walnuts. Pour batter into greased, floured, 12-cup (3 L) bundt cake pan. Bake for 50 to 55 minutes or until cake tester comes out clean.

◆ Cool in pan for 10 minutes, then turn onto cooling rack. Cool and ice with *Brown Sugar Glaze*.

BROWN SUGAR GLAZE:	
¼ CUP (½ STICK) BUTTER	60 ML
¼ CUP PACKED BROWN SUGAR	60 ML
2 TABLESPOONS MILK	30 ML
1 TEASPOON VANILLA	5 ML
1 CUP POWDERED SUGAR	250 ML

◆ In small saucepan, combine butter, brown sugar and milk. Bring to a boil, stirring frequently. Remove from heat, stir in vanilla and beat in powdered sugar.

◆ Cool for several minutes and spoon over cake and let icing run down sides.

CRANBERRY-ORANGE BUNDT CAKE

1 (18 OUNCE) BUTTER RECIPE GOLDEN CAKE MIX	1 (520 G)
3 EGGS	3
⅔ CUP ORANGE JUICE	160 ML
½ CUP (1 STICK) BUTTER, SOFTENED	125 ML
¼ CUP SUGAR	60 ML
1 (8 OUNCE) PACKAGE CREAM CHEESE, SOFTENED	1 (228 G)
ZEST OF 1 MEDIUM ORANGE	1
1 ½ CUPS DRIED SWEETENED CRANBERRIES	375 ML
1 TABLESPOON FLOUR	15 ML

◆ Preheat oven to 350° (176° C). In large bowl, combine cake mix, eggs, orange juice, butter and sugar. Beat on low speed to blend.

◆ Add cream cheese and orange zest and beat for 2 minutes.

◆ In medium bowl, toss cranberries with flour to coat and stir into batter.

◆ Pour batter into greased, floured, 12-cup (3 L) bundt cake pan and bake for 50 to 55 minutes or until cake tester comes out clean.

◆ Cool in pan for 10 minutes, then turn out onto serving plate. When completely cool, top with *Orange Glaze* on next page.

(CONTINUED ON NEXT PAGE.)

For Orange Zest, see page 10.

(CONTINUED)

ORANGE GLAZE:

½ **CUP SUGAR**	**125 ML**
½ **CUP WATER**	**125 ML**
1 ½ **TABLESPOONS CORNSTARCH**	**12 ML**
PINCH SALT	
1 ½ **TABLESPOONS ORANGE ZEST**	**38 ML**
1 **TABLESPOON BUTTER**	**15 ML**
¼ **CUP ORANGE JUICE**	**60 ML**

◆ In medium saucepan, combine sugar, water, cornstarch and salt.

◆ Cook over medium heat, stirring frequently, until mixture comes to a boil. Boil for 1 minute, stirring constantly.

◆ Remove from heat and stir in orange zest and butter. Gradually stir in orange juice.

◆ Return to medium heat, simmer and cook for 3 to 4 minutes until it thickens.

◆ Remove from heat and cool. Spoon over cooled cake.

ORANGE-WALNUT COFFEE CAKE

1 (18 OUNCE) YELLOW CAKE MIX	1 (520 G)
3 EGGS	3
1 (8 OUNCE) CONTAINER SOUR CREAM	1 (228 G)
⅓ CUP ORANGE JUICE	80 ML
ZEST OF 1 LARGE ORANGE	1
½ CUP CHOPPED WALNUTS	125 ML

◆ Preheat oven to 350° (176° C). Mix cake mix, eggs, sour cream, orange juice and orange zest on low speed to blend and beat on medium for 2 minutes.

◆ Gently stir walnuts into batter. Pour batter into greased, floured, 12-cup (3 L) bundt cake pan.

◆ Bake for 40 to 45 minutes or until cake tester comes out clean.

◆ Cool in pan for 10 minutes, then turn onto cooling rack. When cool, spoon *Orange Icing* over top.

ORANGE ICING:

2 TABLESPOONS BUTTER, SOFTENED	30 ML
1 CUP POWDERED SUGAR, DIVIDED	250 ML
2 TABLESPOONS ORANGE JUICE	30 ML
1 TEASPOON ORANGE ZEST	5 ML

◆ In small bowl, cream butter with half powdered sugar. Add orange juice and zest and mix well. Gradually beat in remaining powdered sugar until icing is smooth.

◆ Drizzle icing over top. (The icing will have a somewhat thin consistency, which allows it to flow down sides of the cake.)

For orange zest, see page 10.

COCONUT CAKE

1 (18 OUNCE) BOX WHITE CAKE MIX	**1 (520 G)**
1 (3 OUNCE) COCONUT CREAM PUDDING MIX	**1 (85 G)**
4 EGGS	**4**
2 TABLESPOONS VEGETABLE OIL	**30 ML**
1 CUP CREAM OF COCONUT	**250 ML**
¾ CUP MILK	**180 ML**
2 CUPS SHREDDED COCONUT	**500 ML**

◆ Preheat oven to 350° (176° C). Combine cake mix, pudding mix, eggs, oil, cream of coconut and milk on low speed for 30 seconds, then beat on medium for 2 minutes.

◆ Fold in coconut and pour into greased, floured, 12-cup (3 L) bundt pan.

◆ Bake for 1 hour or until cake tests done. Cool cake and ice with *Chocolate Glaze*.

CHOCOLATE GLAZE:	
6 OUNCES SWEET BAKING CHOCOLATE	**170 G**
SCANT ⅓ CUP WHIPPING CREAM	**80 ML**
2 TABLESPOONS CORN SYRUP	**30 ML**
1 TABLESPOON SUGAR	**15 ML**

◆ In small saucepan, melt chocolate, cream, corn syrup and sugar over low heat until they blend.

◆ Remove from heat and cool slightly. Drizzle over cake.

FRUIT COCKTAIL STREUSEL CAKE

STREUSEL MIXTURE:

½ CUP FLOUR	125 ML
1 CUP SHREDDED COCONUT	250 ML
1 CUP QUICK-COOKING OATS	250 ML
¾ CUP PACKED BROWN SUGAR	180 ML
½ CUP CHOPPED PECANS	125 ML
½ CUP (1 STICK) BUTTER, SOFTENED	125 ML

CAKE:

1 (18 OUNCE) BUTTER RECIPE GOLDEN CAKE MIX	1 (520 G)
1 (3 OUNCE) PACKAGE LEMON INSTANT PUDDING MIX	1 (85 G)
1 (16 OUNCE) CAN FRUIT COCKTAIL WITH SYRUP	1 (454 G)
4 EGGS	4
¼ CUP VEGETABLE OIL	60 ML

◆ Preheat oven to 325° (163° C). In medium bowl combine flour, coconut, oats, brown sugar and pecans. Mix well.

◆ Cut in butter until mixture is crumbly. Set aside.

◆ In large bowl, combine cake mix, pudding mix, syrup from fruit cocktail, eggs and oil.

◆ Beat on medium high speed for 3 minutes. Gently fold in fruit and mix well.

◆ Pour one-third batter into greased, floured, 12-cup (3 L) bundt cake pan. Sprinkle one-third streusel mixture over top. Repeat twice ending with streusel mixture.

◆ Bake for 1 hour or until cake tester comes out clean. Cool cake in pan for 10 minutes, then turn onto cooling rack. When cool, spoon *Butter Glaze* on next page over top.

(CONTINUED ON NEXT PAGE.)

(CONTINUED)

BUTTER GLAZE:

½ CUP (1 STICK) BUTTER	125 ML
½ CUP SUGAR	125 ML
½ CUP EVAPORATED MILK	125 ML
1 CUP SHREDDED COCONUT	250 ML

◆ In small saucepan, combine butter, sugar and evaporated milk. Bring to a boil.

◆ Add coconut and boil for 5 to 6 minutes, stirring frequently, until it thickens. Remove from heat and cool slightly. Drizzle over cake.

APPLE CIDER BUNDT CAKE

1 (18 OUNCE) YELLOW CAKE MIX	1 (520 G)
½ CUP BUTTER, MELTED	125 ML
3 EGGS	3
1 ⅓ CUPS APPLE CIDER	310 ML
1 TEASPOON CINNAMON	5 ML
½ TEASPOON ALLSPICE	2 ML

◆ Preheat oven to 350° (176° C). In large bowl, combine cake mix, butter, eggs, cider, cinnamon and allspice. Beat on low speed to blend, then beat on medium for 2 minutes.

◆ Pour batter into greased, floured, 12-cup (3 L) bundt cake pan and bake for 45 to 50 minutes or until cake tester comes out clean.

◆ Cool in pan for 10 minutes, then turn onto serving platter or cooling rack.

WATERGATE CAKE

1 (18 OUNCE) BOX WHITE CAKE MIX	**1 (520 G)**
1 (3 OUNCE) PACKAGE PISTACHIO INSTANT	
PUDDING MIX	**1 (85 G)**
½ CUP VEGETABLE OIL	**125 ML**
½ CUP MILK	**125 ML**
4 EGGS	**4**
1 (8 OUNCE) CAN CRUSHED PINEAPPLE	
WITH JUICE	**1 (228 G)**
1 CUP MINI-MARSHMALLOWS	**250 ML**
½ CUP CHOPPED PECANS	**125 ML**
½ CUP SHREDDED COCONUT	**125 ML**

◆ Preheat oven to 350° (176° C). In large bowl, combine cake mix, pudding mix, oil, milk, eggs and pineapple with juice.

◆ Beat on low speed for 30 seconds to blend, then beat on medium for 2 minutes.

◆ Gently stir in marshmallows, pecans and coconut.

◆ Pour batter into greased, floured, 12-cup (3 L) bundt pan and bake for 45 to 50 minutes or until cake tests done.

If desired, serve with a dollop of whipped cream.

STRAWBERRY BUNDT CAKE

1 (8 OUNCE) PACKAGE CREAM CHEESE, SOFTENED	1 (228 G)
⅓ CUP SUGAR	80 ML
4 EGGS, DIVIDED	4
1 TEASPOON LEMON EXTRACT	5 ML
1 (18 OUNCE) WHITE CAKE MIX	1 (520 G)
1 (10 OUNCE) CONTAINER SWEETENED STRAWBERRIES WITH JUICE	1 (284 G)
½ CUP SOUR CREAM	125 ML
2 TABLESPOONS VEGETABLE OIL	30 ML
¼ CUP POWDERED SUGAR, OPTIONAL	60 ML

◆ Preheat oven to 350° (176° C). In small bowl, cream cheese with sugar until they blend well. Beat in 1 egg and lemon extract. Set aside.

◆ In large bowl, combine cake mix, strawberry juice, remaining eggs, sour cream and oil. Beat on low speed to blend. Beat on medium speed for 2 minutes.

◆ Add strawberries and gently mix into batter. Pour batter into greased, floured, 12-cup (3 L) bundt cake pan.

◆ Pour cream cheese mixture over center of batter and avoid sides of pan. Gently swirl mixture through batter with knife, but do not over mix.

◆ Bake for 40 to 50 minutes or until cake tester comes out clean. Cool cake in pan for 10 minutes, then turn onto cooling rack. Dust with powdered sugar for decoration.

APPLE COFFEE CAKE

FILLING:

1½ CUPS BAKING APPLES, PEELED, CHOPPED	375 ML
1 TABLESPOON FLOUR	15 ML
¼ TEASPOON NUTMEG	1 ML
⅓ CUP PACKED BROWN SUGAR	80 ML
2 TABLESPOONS BUTTER	30 ML
⅛ TEASPOON SALT	.5 ML
½ CUP GROUND OR FINELY CHOPPED PECANS	125 ML

CAKE:

1 (18 OUNCE) YELLOW CAKE MIX	1 (520 G)
1 (3 OUNCE) PACKAGE VANILLA INSTANT PUDDING MIX	1 (85 G)
4 EGGS	4
1 (8 OUNCE) CONTAINER SOUR CREAM	1 (228 G)
½ CUP VEGETABLE OIL	125 ML

◆ Place all filling ingredients except pecans in medium saucepan. Cook over medium heat, stirring constantly, until apples are tender (about 3 to 4 minutes). Stir in nuts and cool.

◆ Preheat oven to 350° (176° C). In large bowl, combine cake mix, pudding mix, eggs, sour cream and oil. Beat on low speed to blend, then beat on medium for 2 minutes.

◆ Spread one-third batter into greased, floured, 12-cup (3 L) bundt cake pan. Sprinkle half filling mixture evenly over top.

◆ Spread another one-third batter over filling and sprinkle remaining filling on top. Spread remaining batter over top.

(CONTINUED ON NEXT PAGE.)

(CONTINUED)

◆ Bake for 45 to 50 minutes or until cake tester comes out clean. Cool in pan for 10 minutes, then turn onto serving platter.

◆ Sprinkle with powdered sugar or if desired, drizzle *Powdered Sugar Glaze* over top.

POWDERED SUGAR GLAZE:

¾ **CUP POWDERED SUGAR**	**160 ML**
½ **TEASPOON CLEAR VANILLA**	**2 ML**
3 TEASPOONS WARM WATER	**15 ML**

◆ In small bowl, combine sugar and vanilla. Add water, 1 teaspoon at a time until icing reaches drizzling consistency.

◆ Drizzle glaze over cake, use knife to spread more evenly on top of cake and let it run down sides.

◆ You need to work fast, because this icing hardens quickly.

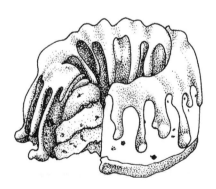

ORANGE-BANANA BUNDT CAKE WITH BUTTERMILK GLAZE

1 (18 OUNCE) YELLOW CAKE MIX	1 (520 G)
1 (8 OUNCE) CONTAINER SOUR CREAM	1 (228 G)
½ CUP VEGETABLE OIL	125 ML
4 EGGS	4
2 TABLESPOONS ORANGE ZEST	30 ML
1 CUP RIPE MASHED BANANAS	250 ML

◆ Preheat oven to 350° (176° C). In large bowl, combine cake mix, sour cream, oil, eggs, orange zest and bananas. Beat on low speed to blend, then beat on medium for 2 minutes.

◆ Pour batter into greased, floured 12-cup (3 L) bundt cake pan. Bake for 50 minutes or until cake tester comes out clean.

◆ Cool in pan for 10 minutes, then turn onto serving platter. Spoon *Buttermilk Glaze* over warm cake.

BUTTERMILK GLAZE:

½ CUP SUGAR	125 ML
¼ CUP BUTTERMILK	60 ML
¼ CUP (½ STICK) BUTTER	60 ML
½ TEASPOON VANILLA	2 ML
2 TEASPOONS CORN SYRUP	10 ML

◆ Combine all ingredients in medium saucepan and bring to simmer over medium heat. Cook for 5 minutes, stirring constantly. Remove from heat and cool slightly.

Start making Buttermilk Glaze the last 20 minutes cake is baking. It will be ready for the cake when you remove it from the pan and ready to eat much sooner.

To make buttermilk and for orange zest, see page 10.

STRAWBERRY-BANANA CAKE

1 (18 OUNCE) FRENCH VANILLA CAKE MIX	1 (520 G)
1 (3 OUNCE) VANILLA INSTANT PUDDING MIX	1 (85 G)
4 EGGS	4
1 CUP MASHED BANANAS	250 ML
½ CUP VEGETABLE OIL	125 ML
1 (10 OUNCE) CONTAINER SWEETENED	
STRAWBERRIES IN SYRUP	1 (284 G)

◆ Preheat oven to 350° (176° C). In large bowl, combine cake mix, pudding mix, eggs, bananas, oil and strawberry syrup.

◆ Beat on low speed to blend, then beat on medium for 2 to 3 minutes until batter thoroughly blends.

◆ Gently stir in strawberries, but be careful not to obliterate them. Pour batter into greased, floured, 12-cup (3 L) bundt cake pan.

◆ Bake for 45 to 50 minutes or until cake tester comes out clean. Cool cake in pan for 10 minutes, then turn onto cooling rack. When cool, spoon *Strawberry Topping* over top.

STRAWBERRY TOPPING:	
1 TABLESPOON CORNSTARCH	15 ML
2 TABLESPOONS ORANGE LIQUEUR OR	30 ML
1 TEASPOON ORANGE EXTRACT AND	5 ML
1 ½ TABLESPOONS WATER	38 ML
2 CUPS FRESH STRAWBERRIES, SLICED	500 ML
½ CUP SUGAR	125 ML
¼ CUP ORANGE JUICE	60 ML

◆ Dissolve cornstarch in orange liqueur. Combine strawberries, sugar and orange juice in small saucepan and cook over medium heat until strawberries are soft (about 10 minutes).

◆ Stir in cornstarch mixture and continue to cook until it thickens (about 4 minutes). Remove from heat, cool and cover top.

FUZZY CATERPILLAR CAKE

1 (18 OUNCE) WHITE CAKE MIX	1 (520 G)
1 (3 OUNCE) PACKAGE VANILLA INSTANT	
PUDDING MIX	1 (85 G)
1 ¼ CUPS MILK	310 ML
4 EGGS	4
⅓ CUP VEGETABLE OIL	80 ML

◆ Preheat oven to 350° (176° C). In large bowl, combine cake mix, pudding mix, milk, eggs and oil. Beat on low speed to blend, then beat on medium for 2 minutes.

◆ Pour batter into greased, floured, 12-cup (3 L) bundt cake pan. Bake for 50 to 55 minutes or until cake tester comes out clean.

◆ Cool cake in pan for 10 minutes, then turn onto cooling rack.

◆ When cool, cut cake in half so that you have 2 semi-circles. Place side of 1 semi-circle against cut side of other semi-circle to make an "s" shape.

◆ Cut corners off front of cake to give the "head" a rounded shape. Frost cake with *Boiled White Icing* and sprinkle with colored coconut. (See page 83.)

◆ In order to make the caterpillar's "feet", cut gumdrops in half vertically and space them evenly apart on either side of cake.

◆ Place 2 chocolate chips, 1 on either side of head for "eyes".

(CONTINUED ON NEXT PAGE.)

(CONTINUED)

BOILED WHITE ICING:

2 EGG WHITES	**2**
1 CUP SUGAR	**250 ML**
⅓ CUP WATER	**80 ML**
¼ TEASPOON CREAM OF TARTAR	**1 ML**
PINCH SALT	
1 TEASPOON CLEAR VANILLA	**5 ML**

◆ Place egg whites in large bowl. Set aside.

◆ In medium saucepan, combine sugar, water, cream of tartar and salt. Bring to a boil, stirring frequently until sugar dissolves.

◆ Remove from heat and slowly add to egg whites in bowl, beating constantly with mixer until stiff peaks form.

◆ Beat in vanilla. Frosting will be very light and fluffy.

GARNISH:

1 CUP SHREDDED COCONUT	**250 ML**
4 DROPS LIQUID FOOD COLOR	**4**
14 GUMDROPS, CUT IN HALF VERTICALLY	
(FOR LEGS)	**14**
2 ROUND CANDIES OR CHOCOLATE CHIPS	
(FOR EYES)	**2**

◆ In medium bowl, combine coconut and food color. Stir well until coconut is colored evenly. (See instruction on page 82 to make "caterpillar".)

GINGER CAKE

1 (18 OUNCE) BUTTER RECIPE GOLDEN CAKE MIX	**1 (520 G)**
⅓ CUP SUGAR	**80 ML**
1 CUP SOUR CREAM	**250 ML**
½ CUP VEGETABLE OIL	**125 ML**
4 EGGS	**4**
1 TEASPOON GROUND GINGER	**5 ML**
1 TABLESPOON FLOUR	**15 ML**
½ CUP CRYSTALLIZED GINGER, MINCED	**125 ML**

◆ Preheat oven to 350° (176° C). In large bowl, combine cake mix, sugar, sour cream, vegetable oil, eggs and ground ginger.

◆ Beat on low speed to blend, then beat on medium for 2 minutes.

◆ In separate bowl, combine flour with ginger; toss to coat. Stir gently into batter.

◆ Pour batter into greased, floured, 12-cup (3 L) bundt cake pan. Bake for 50 to 55 minutes or until cake tester comes out clean.

◆ Cool cake in pan for 10 minutes, then turn onto cooling rack. Serve with whipped cream.

RASPBERRY SOUR CREAM CAKE

1 (18 OUNCE) BUTTER RECIPE GOLDEN CAKE MIX	1 (520 G)
⅓ CUP SUGAR	80 ML
1 CUP SOUR CREAM	250 ML
½ CUP VEGETABLE OIL	125 ML
4 EGGS	4
1 (10 OUNCE) CONTAINER SWEETENED	
RASPBERRIES WITH SYRUP	1 (284 G)

◆ Do not preheat oven. In large bowl, combine cake mix, sugar, sour cream, oil and eggs. Beat on low speed to blend, then beat on medium for 4 minutes.

◆ Pour two-thirds of batter into greased, floured, 12-cup (3 L) bundt cake pan. Drain ¼ cup (60 mL) syrup from raspberries and set aside. Throw away excess syrup.

◆ Drop raspberries on top and top with remaining batter. Place in cold oven and set temperature to 325° (163° C). Bake for 50 to 55 minutes or until cake tester comes out clean.

◆ Cool cake in pan for 10 minutes, then turn onto cooling rack. When cool, spoon *Raspberry Glaze* over top.

RASPBERRY GLAZE:

2 CUPS POWDERED SUGAR	500 ML
¼ CUP RESERVED RASPBERRY SYRUP	60 ML
¼ TEASPOON LEMON EXTRACT	1 ML

◆ Gradually stir raspberry syrup into powdered sugar and blend well after each addition. Stir in lemon extract.

MARBLED BANANA-CHOCOLATE LAYER CAKE

1 (18 OUNCE) WHITE CAKE MIX	**1 (520 G)**
1 CUP MILK	**250 ML**
3 EGGS	**3**
⅓ CUP VEGETABLE OIL	**80 ML**
¼ CUP SUGAR	**60 ML**
½ CUP MASHED BANANAS	**125 ML**
1 CUP SEMI-SWEET CHOCOLATE CHIPS, MELTED	**250 ML**

◆ Preheat oven to 350° (176° C). In large bowl, combine cake mix, milk, eggs, oil and sugar. Beat on low speed to blend, then beat on medium for 2 minutes.

◆ Remove 2 cups (500 mL) batter to medium bowl and set aside. Add bananas to remaining batter in large bowl and beat for another 30 seconds or so until blended.

◆ Stir melted chocolate into reserved batter and mix until thoroughly blended.

◆ Divide banana batter evenly between 2 greased, floured round cake pans. Drop chocolate batter by large spoonfuls evenly over banana batter in both pans.

◆ Use butter knife or tip of icing spatula to swirl chocolate batter through banana batter and be careful not to over mix.

◆ Bake for 30 minutes or until cake tester comes out clean. Let cakes cool in pans for 10 minutes, then turn onto cooling rack. Ice with *Chocolate-Fudge Icing* on next page.

(CONTINUED ON NEXT PAGE.)

(CONTINUED)

CHOCOLATE-FUDGE ICING:

½ CUP (1 STICK) BUTTER	125 ML
2 TABLESPOONS COCOA POWDER	30 ML
3 TABLESPOONS BUTTERMILK	45 ML
1 TEASPOON VANILLA	5 ML
4 CUPS POWDERED SUGAR	1 ML

◆ Melt butter in medium saucepan over medium-high heat.

◆ Add cocoa powder and buttermilk. Bring to a boil, stirring constantly. Remove from heat.

◆ Add vanilla and sugar, 1 cup (250 mL) at a time, beating after each addition. Immediately frost cake before icing starts to harden.

OATMEAL-SPICE CAKE
WITH BROWN SUGAR FROSTING

1 ¼ CUPS WATER	310 ML
1 CUP QUICK-COOKING OATS	250 ML
1 (18 OUNCE) SPICE CAKE MIX	1 (520 G)
4 EGGS	4
⅓ CUP VEGETABLE OIL	80 ML
½ CUP MILK	125 ML

◆ Preheat oven to 350° (176° C). Boil water and combine with oats in medium bowl; stir well and set aside to cool slightly.

◆ In large bowl, combine cake mix, eggs, oil and milk. Beat on low speed to blend, then beat on medium speed for 2 minutes. Add cooled oatmeal and beat for 1 minute more.

◆ Divide batter between 2 greased, floured round cake pans. Bake for 30 to 35 minutes or until cakes test done. When cool, frost with *Brown Sugar Frosting*.

BROWN SUGAR FROSTING:

½ CUP (1 STICK) BUTTER	125 ML
1 ½ CUPS PACKED DARK BROWN SUGAR	375 ML
½ CUP MILK	125 ML
3 ½ CUPS POWDERED SUGAR	875 ML
1 TEASPOON VANILLA	5 ML

◆ In medium saucepan, melt butter and brown sugar. Bring to a boil, stirring constantly, and slowly add milk.

◆ Bring mixture back to a boil and boil for 2 minutes. Remove from heat and cool.

◆ Stir in powdered sugar and vanilla. Beat until smooth and of spreading consistency. Add to cake.

BLACKBERRY JAM CAKE WITH CREAM CHEESE FROSTING

1 (18 OUNCE) WHITE CAKE MIX	**1 (520 G)**
3 EGGS	**3**
⅓ CUP VEGETABLE OIL	**80 ML**
½ CUP PLUS ⅓ CUP SEEDLESS BLACKBERRY JAM	**125 ML + 80 ML**
1 CUP BUTTERMILK	**250 ML**
½ TEASPOON CINNAMON	**2 ML**
½ TEASPOON ALLSPICE	**2 ML**
¼ TEASPOON NUTMEG	**1 ML**

◆ Preheat oven to 350° (176° C). In large bowl, combine all ingredients except ⅓ cup (80 mL) jam and beat on low speed until blended. Beat on medium to high speed for 2 minutes, then divide batter between 2 greased, floured round cake pans.

◆ Bake for 25 to 30 minutes or until cakes test done. Cool and frost with *Cream Cheese Icing*. If you want to fill the layers with jam, use ⅓ cup (80 mL) jam and instructions below.

CREAM CHEESE ICING:

½ CUP (1 STICK) BUTTER	**125 ML**
1 (8 OUNCE) PACKAGE CREAM CHEESE, SOFTENED	**1 (228 G)**
1 TABLESPOON MILK OR HALF-AND-HALF	**15 ML**
1 TEASPOON VANILLA	**5 ML**
1 (1 POUND) BOX POWDERED SUGAR	**1 (454 G)**

◆ In medium bowl, cream butter and cheese until light and fluffy. Beat in milk and vanilla; add powdered sugar, 2 cups (500 mL) at a time and blend well after each addition until icing is smooth.

FOR JAM FILLING

A jam filling really enhances the flavor. In order to keep it from seeping out the sides and discoloring the icing, take some icing on the tip of a knife and spread it in a ring ½ inch from the edge of the cake layer and about ¼ inch deep. Spread jam within this icing ring, place second cake layer on top and frost top and sides of cake.

89

BANANA LAYER CAKE
WITH BUTTER-PECAN FROSTING

1 (18 OUNCE) YELLOW CAKE MIX	1 (520 G)
3 EGGS	3
⅓ CUP VEGETABLE OIL	80 ML
½ CUP PACKED LIGHT BROWN SUGAR	125 ML
1 CUP MILK	250 ML
1 CUP MASHED RIPE BANANAS	250 ML
1 CUP COARSELY CHOPPED PECANS,	
TOASTED, OPTIONAL	250 ML

◆ Preheat oven to 350° (176° C). In large bowl, combine cake mix, eggs, oil, sugar and milk.

◆ Beat on low speed to blend, then beat on medium for 2 minutes.

◆ Add bananas and beat for 1 more minute on medium speed. If desired, stir in pecans.

◆ Divide batter between 2 greased, floured round cake pans.

◆ Bake for 30 to 35 minutes or until cake tester comes out clean.

◆ Cool and frost with *Butter-Pecan Frosting* on next page.

(CONTINUED ON NEXT PAGE.)

Tip: About 2½ bananas equal 1 cup (250 mL) mashed.

(CONTINUED)

BUTTER-PECAN FROSTING:

½ CUP (1 STICK) BUTTER	125 ML
6 CUPS POWDERED SUGAR, DIVIDED	1.5 ML
4 TABLESPOONS LIGHT CREAM	60 ML
1 TEASPOON VANILLA	5 ML
½ TEASPOON BUTTER FLAVORING	2 ML
1 CUP CHOPPED PECANS, TOASTED	250 ML

◆ In large bowl, blend butter, 2 cups (500 mL) powdered sugar, cream, vanilla and butter flavoring until smooth.

◆ Add remaining powdered sugar in several additions and mix well after each addition. Stir in pecans. Frost cake.

TOASTING PECANS

To toast pecans place them on cookie sheet and bake for 8 to 10 minutes at 300° (149° C). Remove when they are light brown. (Watch closely to be sure they don't burn.)

ZUCCHINI CAKE WITH LEMON CREAM CHEESE FROSTING

1 (18 OUNCE) SPICE CAKE MIX	**1 (520 G)**
1 TEASPOON CINNAMON	**5 ML**
½ TEASPOON NUTMEG	**2 ML**
3 EGGS	**3**
⅓ CUP VEGETABLE OIL	**80 ML**
2 TEASPOONS FRESH LEMON JUICE	**10 ML**
¼ CUP ORANGE JUICE	**60 ML**
¼ CUP HONEY	**60 ML**
2 CUPS FINELY GRATED ZUCCHINI	**500 ML**
½ CUP COARSELY CHOPPED WALNUTS, OPTIONAL	**125 ML**

◆ Preheat oven to 350° (176° C). In large bowl, combine cake mix, cinnamon and nutmeg.

◆ Add eggs, oil, lemon juice, orange juice and honey. Mix on low speed to blend, then beat on medium for 2 minutes.

◆ Stir in zucchini and walnuts, if desired.

◆ Divide batter between 2 greased, floured round cake pans. Bake for 30 to 35 minutes, or until cakes test done.

◆ Cool and frost with Lemon *Cream Cheese Frosting* on next page.

(CONTINUED ON NEXT PAGE.)

(CONTINUED)

Lemon Cream Cheese Frosting:

1 (8 OUNCE) PACKAGE CREAM CHEESE, SOFTENED	1 (228 G)
½ CUP (1 STICK) BUTTER, SOFTENED	125 ML
1 TEASPOON LEMON EXTRACT	5 ML
1 TEASPOON VANILLA	5 ML
4½ TO 5 CUPS POWDERED SUGAR	1 L TO
	1.25 ML
½ CUP CHOPPED PECANS, TOASTED*	125 ML

◆ In medium bowl, mix cream cheese, butter, lemon extract and vanilla until thoroughly blended.

◆ Add powdered sugar slowly, mixing well after each addition, until mixture reaches spreading consistency. Stir in pecans. Frost cake.

*See tip on Toasting Pecans on page 10.

COOKIES AND CREAM LAYER CAKE

1 (18 OUNCES) WHITE CAKE MIX	1 (520 G)
½ CUP (4 OUNCES) SOUR CREAM	125 ML
¾ CUP MILK	180 ML
3 EGG WHITES	3
2 TABLESPOONS VEGETABLE OIL	30 ML
2 CUPS CRUSHED CHOCOLATE-SANDWICH COOKIES, DIVIDED	500 ML

◆ Preheat oven to 350° (176° C). In large mixing bowl, combine cake mix, sour cream, milk, egg whites and oil.

◆ Beat on low speed to blend, then beat on medium for 2 to 3 minutes.

◆ Stir 1½ cups (375 mL) crushed cookies into batter. Divide batter between 2 greased, floured round cake pans.

◆ Bake for 30 to 35 minutes or until cake tester comes out clean. Cool and frost with *White Frosting* on next page, then sprinkle remaining ½ cup (125 mL) crushed cookies on top of cake for decoration.

(CONTINUED)

WHITE FROSTING:

½ CUP MILK	125 ML
1 TABLESPOON CORNSTARCH	15 ML
½ CUP VEGETABLE SHORTENING	125 ML
4 CUPS POWDERED SUGAR, DIVIDED	1 L
1 ½ TEASPOONS VANILLA	7 ML

◆ Blend milk and cornstarch. Place in small saucepan and cook over low heat, stirring constantly, until mixture thickens.

◆ Remove from heat and cool.

◆ In medium bowl, cream shortening with 1 cup (250 mL) powdered sugar until mixture is light and fluffy. Add milk mixture and blend well.

◆ Stir in vanilla and remaining powdered sugar 1 cup (250 mL) at a time, mixing well after each addition, until frosting is spreading consistency. Frost cake.

To crush cookies for this cake, I use a sealable plastic bag. Place cookies in bag and use a rolling pin to crush them by gently pounding them or rolling over them. Be careful not to pulverize the cookies. I like to have them coarsely broken, not smashed beyond recognition.

AUTUMN SPICE CAKE

1 (18 OUNCE) SPICE CAKE MIX	1 (520 G)
1 (1 POUND) CAN PUMPKIN	1 (454 G)
3 EGGS	3
⅓ CUP ORANGE JUICE	80 ML
1 TEASPOON CINNAMON	5 ML

◆ Preheat oven to 350° (176° C). Combine all ingredients and beat on low speed for 30 seconds to blend. Beat on high speed for 2 minutes.

◆ Divide batter between 2 greased, floured round cake pans and bake for 25 or 30 minutes or until cakes test done.

◆ Cool and frost with *Maple Cream Cheese* frosting on next page.

MAPLE CREAM CHEESE FROSTING:

¼ CUP (½ STICK) BUTTER	60 ML
1 (8 OUNCE) PACKAGE CREAM CHEESE, SOFTENED	1 (228 G)
¼ CUP MAPLE SYRUP	60 ML
4 CUPS POWDERED SUGAR	1 L

◆ With mixer on low, blend butter and cream cheese. Add maple syrup and mix well.

◆ Slowly add powdered sugar, beating after each addition, until well blended. Frost cake.

The icing for this Autumn Spice Cake really enhances the pumpkin and spice flavors. For the best flavor, I use real maple syrup. Its intense flavor can't be matched by the artificial maple syrups.

DEVIL'S FOOD CREAM CHEESE CAKE

1 (8 OUNCE) PACKAGE CREAM CHEESE, SOFTENED	1 (228 G)
⅓ CUP SUGAR	80 ML
4 EGGS, DIVIDED	4
1 TEASPOON VANILLA	5 ML
1 (18 OUNCE) DEVIL'S FOOD CAKE MIX	1 (520 G)
1 CUP BUTTERMILK	250 ML
⅓ CUP VEGETABLE OIL	80 ML

◆ Preheat oven to 350° (176° C). In small bowl, cream cheese with sugar until blended. Beat in 1 egg and vanilla until mixture is light and fluffy.

◆ In large bowl, combine cake mix with buttermilk, oil and remaining eggs. Beat on low speed to blend, then beat on medium for 2 minutes.

◆ Divide batter between 2 greased, floured round cake pans. Divide cream cheese mixture evenly between the cakes, dropping by spoonsful onto batter.

◆ Gently swirl it with knife or spatula to create a marbled effect. Bake for 30 to 35 minutes or until cake tester comes out clean. Cool cakes and frost with *Fudge Frosting*.

FUDGE FROSTING:

4 OUNCES UNSWEETENED CHOCOLATE, MELTED	115 G
½ CUP (1 STICK) BUTTER, MELTED	125 ML
½ CUP WHIPPING CREAM	125 ML
1 (1 POUND) BOX POWDERED SUGAR	1 (454 G)
2 TEASPOONS VANILLA	10 ML

◆ Combine chocolate and butter; stir until well blended. In medium bowl, stir whipping cream into powdered sugar, then stir in vanilla. Add chocolate mixture and beat until completely mixed. If frosting is too thin, place bowl in larger bowl of ice water and continue to beat until mixture reaches frosting consistency.

RED VELVET CAKE

1 (18 OUNCE) WHITE CAKE MIX	1 (520 G)
1 (3 OUNCE) VANILLA INSTANT PUDDING MIX	1 (85 G)
3 TABLESPOONS COCOA	45 ML
4 EGGS	4
1 CUP MILK	250 ML
½ CUP VEGETABLE OIL	125 ML
1 OUNCE RED FOOD COLORING	28 G

◆ Preheat oven to 350° (176° C). In large bowl, combine all ingredients. Beat on low speed to blend, then beat on medium speed for 4 minutes.

◆ Divide batter between 3 greased, floured round cake pans. Bake for 25 to 30 minutes or until cake tester comes out clean. Cool and frost with *Cream Cheese Icing*.

CREAM CHEESE ICING:

¾ CUP (1 ½ STICKS) BUTTER, SOFTENED	180 ML
1 ½ (8 OUNCE) PACKAGES CREAM CHEESE, SOFTENED	1½ (228 G)
1 ½ TEASPOONS VANILLA	7 ML
1 ½ TEASPOONS ALMOND EXTRACT	7 ML
1 ½ TO 2 (1 POUND) BOXES POWDERED SUGAR	1½ TO 2 (454 G)

◆ Cream butter and cream cheese until blended.

◆ Add vanilla and almond extract; gradually add powdered sugar, blending well after each addition. Frost cake.

BLACK WALNUT CAKE

1 (18 OUNCE) BOX WHITE CAKE MIX	1 (520 G)
1⅓ CUPS MILK	330 ML
⅓ CUP WATER	80 ML
2 TABLESPOONS VEGETABLE OIL	30 ML
3 EGGS	3
1 CUP FINELY GROUND BLACK WALNUTS	250 ML

◆ Preheat oven to 350° (176° C). In large bowl, combine cake mix, milk, water, vegetable oil and eggs. Beat on low speed to blend, then beat on medium for 2 minutes more. Stir in black walnuts until well blended.

◆ Divide batter between 2 greased, floured 9-inch (23 cm) round cake pans and bake for 30 minutes or until cake springs back when lightly touched.

◆ Let cakes cool in pans for 10 minutes, then turn onto cooling rack. Ice with *Maple Frosting*.

MAPLE FROSTING:

½ CUP (1 STICK) BUTTER	125 ML
½ CUP PACKED LIGHT BROWN SUGAR	125 ML
½ CUP REAL MAPLE SYRUP	125 ML
¼ CUP MILK	60 ML
2 TO 2½ CUPS POWDERED SUGAR, DIVIDED	500 TO 625 ML

◆ Melt butter in medium saucepan. Add brown sugar and maple syrup and bring to a boil. Boil for 2 minutes, stirring constantly. Add milk and bring back to a boil.

◆ Stir in ¼ cup (60 mL) powdered sugar, remove from heat and cool to lukewarm temperature. Gradually beat in remaining sugar until frosting is spreading consistency. Spread over cake.

CHERRY CAKE

1 (18 OUNCE) WHITE CAKE MIX	1 (520 G)
1 ⅓ CUPS MILK	330 ML
2 TABLESPOONS VEGETABLE OIL	15 ML
3 EGG WHITES	3
¾ CUP WHITE CHOCOLATE CHIPS, MELTED	180 ML
¾ CUP MARASCHINO CHERRIES, WELL DRAINED, COARSELY CHOPPED	180 ML

◆ Preheat oven to 350° (176° C). In large bowl, combine cake mix, milk, oil, egg whites and white chocolate.

◆ Beat on low speed to blend, then beat on medium for 3 minutes. Gently stir in cherries.

◆ Divide batter between 2 greased, floured round cake pans. Bake for 30 to 35 minutes or until cake tester comes out clean. Cool and frost with *Cherry Frosting*.

CHERRY FROSTING:

⅓ CUP MILK	80 ML
3 TABLESPOONS BUTTER, SOFTENED	45 ML
5 TO 6 CUPS POWDERED SUGAR, DIVIDED	1.25 TO 1.5 L
2 TABLESPOONS MARASCHINO CHERRY JUICE	30 ML
6 MARASCHINO CHERRIES, CHOPPED	6

◆ In medium bowl, combine milk, butter and 1 cup (250 mL) powdered sugar. Beat in cherry juice and remaining powdered sugar a little at a time. Fold in chopped cherries. Frost cake.

WATERMELON CAKE WITH LIME FROSTING

1 (3 OUNCE) PACKAGE WATERMELON FLAVOR GELATIN	1 (85 G)
1 CUP WARM WATER	250 ML
1 (18 OUNCE) WHITE CAKE MIX	1 (520 G)
4 EGGS	4
½ CUP VEGETABLE OIL	125 ML
SEVERAL DROPS OF RED FOOD COLORING, OPTIONAL	

◆ Preheat oven to 350° (176° C). In large bowl, stir gelatin into water until it dissolves.

◆ Add cake mix, eggs and oil. (At this point, you can add several drops of red food coloring, if desired, to color the batter a deeper pink or red.) Blend on low speed to moisten, then beat on medium for 2 minutes.

◆ Divide batter between 2 greased, floured round cake pans. Bake for 30 minutes or until cake tester comes out clean. Cool and frost with *Lime Frosting*.

LIME FROSTING:	
½ CUP (1 STICK) BUTTER, SOFTENED	125 ML
3 TO 3 ½ CUPS POWDERED SUGAR	750 TO 875 ML
4 TABLESPOONS FRESH LIME JUICE	60 ML
1 TEASPOON LIME ZEST	5 ML
1 TEASPOON CLEAR VANILLA	5 ML
SEVERAL DROPS OF GREEN FOOD COLORING, OPTIONAL	

◆ In medium bowl, cream butter with 1 cup (250 mL) powdered sugar. Add lime juice, zest and vanilla. Blend well.

◆ Gradually add remaining powdered sugar, beating well after each addition, until frosting reaches spreading consistency. (If desired, add a few drops of green food coloring.) Frost cake.

LUSCIOUS ORANGE TORTE

1 (3 OUNCE) PACKAGE ORANGE INSTANT GELATIN	1 (85 G)
1 CUP ORANGE JUICE	250 ML
1 (18 OUNCE) YELLOW CAKE MIX	1 (520 G)
½ CUP OIL	125 ML
3 EGGS	3

◆ Preheat oven to 350° (176° C). Stir gelatin into orange juice until it dissolves. In large bowl, combine orange juice-gelatin mixture with cake mix, oil and eggs. Beat on low speed to blend, then beat on medium for 3 minutes.

◆ Divide batter between 2 greased, floured round cake pans. Bake for 30 minutes or until cake tester comes out clean.

◆ Let cakes cool slightly in pan, then poke holes ½ inch apart over entire surface of each.

◆ Spoon *Orange Glaze* evenly over top and let allowing glaze soak in. Let cakes sit undisturbed for about 1 hour, then assemble.

◆ Cut each layer in half. Fill first layer with half of filling. Top with second layer and cover with some frosting.

◆ Place third layer on top and fill with remaining filling. Top with fourth layer. Frost cake top and sides with remaining frosting. (Keep refrigerated.)

(CONTINUED ON NEXT PAGE.)

For orange zest, see page 10.

(CONTINUED)

ORANGE GLAZE:
2 CUPS POWDERED SUGAR	**500 ML**
⅔ CUP ORANGE JUICE	**160 ML**
ZEST OF 1 ORANGE	**1**

◆ In small bowl, gradually whisk orange juice into powdered sugar.

◆ Whisk in orange zest. (If not using immediately, stir again just before use, to incorporate zest into glaze before you pour it over the cake.)

FILLING:
1 (14 OUNCE) CAN SWEETENED CONDENSED MILK	**1 (420 G)**
⅓ CUP FRESH LEMON JUICE	**1 (80 ML)**
4 OUNCES FROZEN WHIPPED TOPPING, THAWED	**115 G**

◆ In medium bowl, combine condensed milk and lemon juice; stir until well blended. Fold in whipped topping. Refrigerate until use.

FROSTING
1 (20 OUNCE) CAN CRUSHED PINEAPPLE WITH JUICE	**1 (570 G)**
1 (3 OUNCE) VANILLA INSTANT PUDDING MIX	**1 (85 G)**
1 (8 OUNCE) CONTAINER FROZEN WHIPPED TOPPING, THAWED	**1 (228 G)**

◆ In large bowl, combine pineapple with juice and pudding mix. Stir well. Fold in whipped topping.

BANANA SPLIT TORTE

*This cake is a cinch to put together—the whipped
cream only takes a few minutes to make and
with no frosting to prepare, once the cake cools,
you can quickly create a pretty dessert
with little effort.*

1 (18 OUNCE) WHITE CAKE MIX	1 (520 G)
1 ⅓ CUPS MILK	310 ML
¼ CUP VEGETABLE OIL	60 ML
3 EGGS	3
2 TEASPOONS BUTTER FLAVORING	10 ML
1 CUP MASHED BANANAS	250 ML
1 CUP WHIPPING CREAM	250 ML
2 TABLESPOONS POWDERED SUGAR	30 ML
1 CUP FRESH SLICED STRAWBERRIES	250 ML
1 (8 OUNCE) CAN CRUSHED PINEAPPLE, DRAINED	1 (228 G)
1 (12 OUNCE) JAR FUDGE ICE CREAM TOPPING	1 (340 G)
¼ CUP CHOPPED NUTS	60 ML

◆ Preheat oven to 350° (176° C). In large bowl, combine cake
mix, milk, oil, eggs, butter flavoring and bananas. Beat on low
speed to blend, then beat on medium for 2 minutes.

◆ Divide batter between 2 greased, floured round cake pans.
Bake for 30 minutes or until cake tester comes out clean. Cool.

◆ While cake is baking (or cooling), prepare the fillings and
refrigerate until cake cools and is ready for assembly.

◆ Beat whipping cream with powdered sugar until stiff peaks form.
Divide in half. Fold strawberries into half of whipped cream. Fold
pineapple into other half.

(CONTINUED ON NEXT PAGE.)

(CONTINUED)

TO ASSEMBLE CAKE:

◆ Warm fudge topping slightly to make it easier to work with. (Warm it in small saucepan over low heat or in microwave at half power, stirring every 30 seconds or so to keep it from getting too hot.)

◆ Split each cake layer horizontally.

◆ Place bottom of 1 layer on serving plate, top with strawberry cream and spread cream evenly over surface. Place second cake layer on top and spoon half fudge topping and let it drip down sides of bottom layer.

◆ Place third layer on top and spread pineapple cream evenly.

◆ Top with fourth layer and spoon remaining fudge topping over top, covering entire surface and letting it drip down the sides. Sprinkle nuts over fudge.

◆ Keep cake refrigerated until ready to serve.

DEEP DARK CHOCOLATE-ORANGE TORTE

1 (18 OUNCE) DEVIL'S FOOD CAKE MIX	1 (520 G)
3 EGGS	3
⅓ CUP VEGETABLE OIL	80 ML
1 ⅓ CUPS BUTTERMILK	310 ML
3 TEASPOONS ORANGE EXTRACT	15 ML

◆ Preheat oven to 350° (176° C). In large bowl, combine cake mix, eggs, oil, buttermilk and orange extract.

◆ Beat on low speed to blend, then beat on medium for 2 minutes.

◆ Divide batter between 2 greased, floured round cake pans and bake for 30 to 35 minutes or until cake tester comes out clean.

◆ Cool cakes and slice each layer in half.

◆ Fill first layer with half of *Orange Filling*, place second layer on top and frost with some *Chocolate Frosting* on next page.

◆ Top with third layer and fill with remaining *Orange Filling*. Place fourth layer on top and frost top and sides with remaining *Chocolate Frosting*.

(CONTINUED ON NEXT PAGE.)

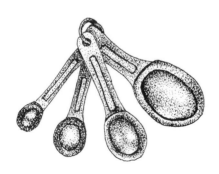

(CONTINUED)

ORANGE FILLING:

1 CUP SUGAR	250 ML
4 TABLESPOONS CORNSTARCH	60 ML
3 TEASPOONS ORANGE ZEST	15 ML
½ TEASPOON SALT	2 ML
1 ½ CUPS ORANGE JUICE	375 ML
½ CUP WATER	125 ML
4 SLIGHTLY BEATEN EGG YOLKS	4
4 TABLESPOONS BUTTER	60 ML

◆ In medium saucepan, combine sugar, cornstarch, orange zest and salt.

◆ Gradually whisk in orange juice, water and egg yolks. Blend well and bring to a simmer and whisk mixture frequently.

◆ Cook over medium heat until thick. Remove from heat. Stir in butter until melted. Cool slightly.

CHOCOLATE FROSTING:

⅓ CUP (5 ⅓ TABLESPOONS) BUTTER	80 ML
⅔ CUP UNSWEETENED COCOA POWDER	160 ML
1 TEASPOON VANILLA	5 ML
⅓ CUP MILK	80 ML
3 CUPS POWDERED SUGAR	625 ML

◆ In medium saucepan, melt butter over medium heat; add cocoa powder, stirring until well blended and mixture starts to boil. Remove from heat.

◆ Add vanilla and half of milk, stirring until well blended. Stir in 1 cup (250 mL) powdered sugar. Stir in remaining milk, add remaining powdered sugar, 1 cup (250 mL) at a time, and beat until frosting is smooth.

If you're short on time, forget the filling and just frost the cake without splitting the layers. It's just as delicious.

PINEAPPLE TORTE

1 (18 OUNCE) WHITE CAKE MIX	**1 (520 G)**
½ CUP RESERVED PINEAPPLE JUICE *	**125 ML**
3 EGGS	**3**
¼ CUP VEGETABLE OIL	**60 ML**
¾ CUP MILK	**180 ML**

◆ Preheat oven to 350° (176° C). In large bowl, combine cake mix, ½ cup (125 mL) pineapple juice from crushed pineapple below, eggs, oil and milk. Beat on low speed to blend, then on medium speed for 3 minutes.

◆ Divide batter between 2 greased, floured round cake pans and bake for 25 to 30 minutes or until cake tests done. Cool cakes and cut each layer in half.

◆ Assemble cake by filling first layer with half of pineapple filling, place second layer on top and fill with about 1 cup (250 mL) *7-Minute Frosting* on next page.

◆ Place third layer on top and fill with remaining pineapple filling. Top with fourth cake layer and frost cake top and sides with remaining frosting.

PINEAPPLE FILLING:	
1 CUP SUGAR	**250 ML**
4 TABLESPOONS FLOUR	**60 ML**
*1 (20 OUNCE) CAN CRUSHED PINEAPPLE WITH	
½ CUP JUICE	**1 (570 G)**
2 EGGS, BEATEN	**2**
2 TABLESPOONS FRESH LEMON JUICE	**30 ML**
1 TABLESPOON BUTTER	**15 ML**
1 TEASPOON VANILLA	**5 ML**

◆ Combine sugar and flour and place in medium saucepan. Add remaining ingredients, and cook over medium heat, stirring constantly until mixture thickens (about 3 to 4 minutes). Remove from heat and let cool.

(CONTINUED ON NEXT PAGE.)

(CONTINUED)

7-MINUTE FROSTING:

1 ½ CUPS SUGAR	375 ML
¼ CUP PLUS 1 TABLESPOON WATER	60 ML + 15 ML
2 EGG WHITES	2
1 TABLESPOON LIGHT CORN SYRUP	15 ML
PINCH OF SALT	
1 TEASPOON VANILLA	5 ML

◆ Combine sugar, water, egg whites, corn syrup and salt in top of double boiler. Beat constantly on high speed over boiling water for 7 minutes. Remove from heat and add vanilla.

◆ Continue beating until stiff peaks form (about 4 more minutes) and frosting reaches spreading consistency.

Clear vanilla is best to use so icing is not discolored.

I like to add a little yellow food coloring to the frosting when I add the vanilla in order to make the icing color match the yellow cake and filling.

If you're not in the mood to make the filling and frosting, just forget the filling and frost the cake layers with the 7-Minute Frosting.

KAHLUA-MOUSSE TORTE

(Otherwise known as "Nana's Midnight Snack Cake")

CAKE:

1 (18	1 (520 G)
OUNCE) DEVIL'S FOOD CAKE MIX	180 ML
¾ CUP KAHLUA	125 ML
½ CUP STRONG COFFEE	3
3 EGGS	125 ML
½ CUP VEGETABLE OIL	

◆ Preheat oven to 350° (176° C). In large mixing bowl, combine cake mix, kahlua, coffee, eggs and oil. Beat on low speed to blend, then beat on medium for 2 minutes more.

◆ Divide batter evenly between 2 greased, floured round baking pans. Bake for 30 to 35 minutes or until cakes test done. Cool completely.

◆ To assemble cake, slice each cake layer in half horizontally and top first layer with one-third of *Chocolate Mousse Filling*. Top with second cake layer with half of *Chocolate Glaze* on next page and let it run down sides of cake. At this point, if possible, refrigerate this layer to set chocolate and mousse for about 1 hour.

◆ Put another third of mousse over chocolate, and top with third cake layer. Cover third layer with remaining mousse and put fourth cake layer on top.

◆ Spoon remaining chocolate glaze over top and let some of it drip over cake edges. Refrigerate immediately.

(CONTINUED ON NEXT PAGE.)

(CONTINUED)

CHOCOLATE MOUSSE FILLING:

4 EGG YOLKS	4
¼ CUP SUGAR	60 ML
2 ½ CUPS WHIPPING CREAM, DIVIDED	625 ML
1 CUP SEMI-SWEET CHOCOLATE CHIPS	250 ML

◆ In small bowl, beat egg yolks on high speed until thick (about 3 minutes). Gradually beat in sugar.

◆ In medium saucepan, heat 1 cup (250 mL) whipping cream over medium heat just until hot (do not boil). Slowly stir some of heated whipping cream into egg and sugar mixture. Return remaining cream in saucepan to heat.

◆ Cook over low heat for 5 minutes, stirring constantly, until mixture thickens. (Do not bring to a boil.)

◆ Add chocolate chips and stir until they melt. Remove from heat. Cover and refrigerate until chilled (about 1 ½ hours).

◆ Beat remaining 1 ½ cups (375 mL) whipping cream on high speed until stiff peaks form. Gently fold chilled chocolate mixture into whipped cream until mixed.

CHOCOLATE GLAZE:

½ CUP WHIPPING CREAM	125 ML
1 CUP SEMI-SWEET CHOCOLATE CHIPS	250 ML

◆ In small saucepan, heat whipping cream and chocolate over medium heat until chocolate melts and mixture is smooth (do not boil).

◆ Remove from heat and cool to room temperature.

CHOCOLATE-BOURBON CAKE WITH PRALINE CREAM

1 (18 OUNCE) SWISS CHOCOLATE CAKE MIX	1 (520 G)
1 (3 OUNCE) CHOCOLATE INSTANT PUDDING MIX	1 (85 G)
½ CUP BOURBON	125 ML
½ CUP VEGETABLE OIL	125 ML
½ CUP BUTTERMILK	125 ML
4 EGGS	4
1 CUP CHOPPED PECANS, TOASTED	250 ML
¼ CUP CARAMEL SAUCE, OPTIONAL	60 ML

◆ Preheat oven to 350° (176° C). In large bowl, combine cake mix, pudding mix, bourbon, oil, buttermilk and eggs.

◆ Beat on low speed to blend, then beat on medium speed for 2 minutes. Stop after 1 minute to scrape bowl.

◆ Stir in pecans and divide batter between 3 greased, floured round cake pans. Bake for 20 to 25 minutes or until cake tester comes out clean.

◆ When cool, fill each layer with one-third praline cream mixture and spread remaining one-third of mixture on top layer.

◆ If desired, drizzle caramel sauce over top and let it drip down cake sides.

(CONTINUED ON NEXT PAGE.)

(CONTINUED)

PRALINE-CREAM MIXTURE:
2 CUPS WHIPPING CREAM	**500 ML**
2 TABLESPOONS POWDERED SUGAR	**30 ML**
⅓ CUP CARAMEL SAUCE*	**80 ML**

◆ In medium bowl, combine whipping cream and powdered sugar.

◆ Beat on high speed with mixer until stiff peaks form. Fold in caramel sauce until well blended.

The Caramel Sauce on page 171 will work here, but if you are in a rush, use prepared caramel sauce.

For added effect, sprinkle candied pecan halves over the top. (See Special Touches on page 16.) They are easy to make and only take a little extra time, but they sure will make the cake look extra delicious.

You may also want to make them from time to time just for a snack. They keep for days in an airtight container.

ORANGE-MERINGUE TORTE
WITH APRICOT FILLING

*Topping your cakes with meringue adds
texture and elegance with very little effort. The
combination of cake, meringue and filling add
up to one impressive, delicious dessert.*

1 (18 OUNCE) YELLOW CAKE MIX	**1 (520 G)**
1 (3 OUNCE) PACKAGE ORANGE GELATIN	**1 (85 G)**
4 EGGS, SEPARATED	**4**
1 CUP ORANGE JUICE	**250 ML**
⅓ CUP VEGETABLE OIL	**80 ML**
PINCH SALT	
1 CUP SUGAR	**250 ML**
1 TEASPOON VANILLA	**5 ML**

◆ Preheat oven to 350° (176° C). In large bowl combine cake mix, gelatin, egg yolks, orange juice and oil. Beat on low speed to blend, then beat on medium for 3 minutes.

◆ Divide batter between 2 greased, floured round cake pans. Set aside while you prepare meringue topping.

(CONTINUED ON NEXT PAGE.)

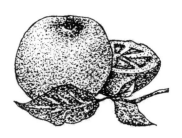

(CONTINUED)

◆ In medium bowl, beat egg whites and salt on high speed until soft peaks form. Add sugar in several additions, beating well after each addition.

◆ Add vanilla and beat until mixture is stiff and glossy. Spread meringue evenly over cake batter in each pan, smooth the surface and spread it to edges of cake pans.

◆ Bake for 35 minutes or until meringue is light brown and cake tester comes out clean. Let cakes cool in pans for 10 minutes, then carefully remove each layer to cooling rack, right side up.

◆ To remove cakes from pans, place a flat plate or your hand over meringue side, turn pan upside down and then gently place cake right side up on rack. The meringue will crack a little, but it is not bad.

◆ When well cooled, spread 1 layer with half of *Apricot Filling* and place other layer on top.

◆ Frost sides of cake with remaining half of filling (leave top meringue layer exposed).

APRICOT FILLING:

1 ½ CUPS WHIPPING CREAM	375 ML
2 TABLESPOONS POWDERED SUGAR	30 ML
¾ CUP APRICOT PRESERVES	180 ML

◆ In medium bowl, beat whipping cream until soft peaks form, then add powdered sugar and beat until stiff. Fold in apricot preserves.

APRICOT TORTE

1 (18 OUNCE) BUTTER RECIPE GOLDEN CAKE MIX	1 (520 G)
½ CUP (1 STICK) BUTTER, SOFTENED	125 ML
3 EGGS	3
⅔ CUP APRICOT SYRUP	
(SEE FILLING RECIPE BELOW.)	160 ML

◆ Preheat oven to 350° (176° C). In large bowl, combine cake mix, butter, eggs and apricot syrup from apricot halves in filling below.

◆ Beat on low speed to blend, then beat on medium for 3 minutes.

◆ Divide batter between 2 greased, floured round cake pans. Bake for 30 minutes or until cake tester comes out clean and cool.

◆ Slice each layer horizontally, then spread *Filling and Frosting*. Keep cake refrigerated.

FILLING AND FROSTING:

1 (8 OUNCE) PACKAGE CREAM CHEESE, SOFTENED	1 (228 G)
1 (14 OUNCE) CAN SWEETENED CONDENSED MILK	1 (420 G)
¼ CUP FRESH LEMON JUICE	60 ML
1 (12 OUNCE) CONTAINER FROZEN	
WHIPPED TOPPING, THAWED	1 (340 G)
1 (16 OUNCE) CAN APRICOT HALVES, CHOPPED	1 (454 G)
PLUS ⅔ CUP SYRUP	160 ML

◆ In large bowl, combine cream cheese and condensed milk. Beat on low to medium speed until smooth.

◆ Stir in lemon juice, then whipped topping. Blend well. Fold in chopped apricots and add to torte.

ALMOND-CHERRY TORTE

1 (18 OUNCE) WHITE CAKE MIX	1 (520 G)
3 EGGS	3
1 ⅓ CUPS BUTTERMILK	310 ML
3 TABLESPOONS VEGETABLE OIL	45 ML
2 TEASPOONS ALMOND EXTRACT	10 ML
1 TABLESPOON FLOUR	15 ML
1 CUP SLICED ALMONDS	250 ML

◆ Preheat oven to 350° (176° C). In large bowl, combine cake mix, eggs, buttermilk, oil and almond extract. Beat on low speed to blend, then beat on medium for 2 minutes.

◆ In small bowl, coat almonds with flour, then stir into batter. Divide batter between 2 greased, floured round cake pans.

◆ Bake for 30 to 35 minutes or until cake tester comes out clean. Cool and frost with *Cherry Filling and Icing*.

CHERRY FILLING AND ICING:

2 ½ CUPS HEAVY WHIPPING CREAM	625 ML
3 TABLESPOONS POWDERED SUGAR	45 ML
2 CUPS CHERRY PRESERVES, DIVIDED	500 ML

◆ In medium bowl, beat whipping cream on high speed until soft peaks form. Add powdered sugar and continue to beat until stiff. Fold in 1 cup (250 mL) cherry preserves.

◆ Slice each cake layer in half. Spread one third whip cream filling on bottom cake layer. Top with second cake layer and spread with 1 cup (250 mL) remaining cherry preserves.

◆ Top with third cake layer and spread one third whip cream filling. Top with fourth cake layer. Spread remaining whip cream filling over top and sides. Refrigerate until ready to serve.

COLOSSAL PETITS FOURS

I have always loved petits fours. I don't know what it is about the tiny little cakes that I like so much—their attractive little colorful decorations, the jam sandwiched between the tasty cake or the rich, satisfying taste of icing, cake and jam in every bite-size morsel.

Here's a larger version made with oversized cookie cutters in fun holiday and specialty shapes.

CAKE:

1 (18 OUNCE) WHITE CAKE MIX	**1 (520 G)**	
1 ⅓ CUPS BUTTERMILK	**310 ML**	
3 EGGS	**3**	
¼ CUP VEGETABLE OIL	**60 ML**	
1 TEASPOON ALMOND EXTRACT	**5 ML**	
JAM FOR FILLING		

◆ Preheat oven to 350° (176° C). In large bowl, combine cake mix, buttermilk, eggs, oil and almond extract.

◆ Beat on low speed to blend, then beat on medium for 2 minutes.

◆ Pour batter into greased, floured jelly-roll pan and bake for 20 to 25 minutes or until cake tester comes out clean.

◆ Turn onto cooling rack until cool, then place on flat surface.

◆ Cut shapes with cookie cutters (your cutters should be about 1½ to 2 inches tall). Slice in half horizontally and fill with thin layer of jam.

(CONTINUED ON NEXT PAGE.)

(CONTINUED)

◆ Place cakes back on cooling rack and put wax paper beneath rack to catch icing drips.

◆ Spoon glaze over cakes and let it run down sides to cover as much as possible. If you'd like, while glaze is still wet, sprinkle colored sugar or candy jimmies top over for decoration.

WHITE CHOCOLATE GLAZE:
½ CUP MILK **125 ML**
¾ CUP WHITE CHOCOLATE CHIPS **180 ML**
4 CUPS POWDERED SUGAR **1 L**

◆ In medium saucepan, heat milk and white chocolate chips over low heat, stirring constantly until chips melt. Remove from heat.

◆ Gradually stir in powdered sugar, beating as you add it, until mixture is smooth.

◆ If desired, tint the glaze by adding a few drops of food coloring, 1 drop at a time. Stir after each addition until glaze reaches the color you want.

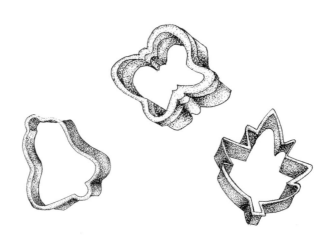

CINNAMON ROLLS

1 (18 OUNCE) YELLOW CAKE MIX	1 (520 G)
5 TO 5 ½ CUPS FLOUR, DIVIDED	1.25 TO 1.5 L
2 (.25 OUNCE) PACKAGES DRY YEAST	2 (.7 G)
2 ½ CUPS WARM (110° F) WATER, DIVIDED	625 ML
½ CUP (1 STICK) BUTTER, SOFTENED	125 ML
1 CUP PACKED BROWN SUGAR	250 ML
4 TEASPOONS CINNAMON	20 ML
1 CUP FINELY CHOPPED PECANS	250 ML

◆ In large bowl, combine cake mix and 3 cups (750 mL) flour; stir to mix thoroughly.

◆ In medium bowl, stir yeast into ½ cup (125 mL) warm water. Add to cake and flour mixture. Add remaining 2 cups (500 mL) warm water, and mix into dough.

◆ Add remaining 2 to 2 ½ cups (500 to 625 mL) flour to make dough pliable. (You'll want the dough to be workable, not sticky.) If necessary, add a little more flour to get consistency right. Cover and let rise until doubled in size (about 1 hour). (Tips for helping dough rise are on page 123.)

◆ In small bowl, mix butter, sugar, cinnamon and pecans.

◆ Divide dough in half. Roll one half into rectangle about ½ inch thick. Spread half sugar mixture evenly over dough and roll dough from long side.

◆ Cut into ½-inch thick slices and place on greased cookie sheet, cut side down with sides touching. Repeat with other half dough.

(CONTINUED ON NEXT PAGE.)

(CONTINUED)

◆ Cover rolls and set aside to rise again until double in size. Bake at 375° (190° C) for 10 to 15 minutes.

◆ Remove from oven and drizzle with Powdered Sugar Icing.

POWDERED SUGAR ICING:

2 CUPS POWDERED SUGAR	500 ML
1 TEASPOON CLEAR VANILLA	5 ML
3 TABLESPOONS WARM WATER	45 ML

◆ In small bowl, combine above ingredients and stir until well blended and drizzling consistency.

CREAM CHEESE FILLED COFFEE CAKE ROLLS

PASTRY DOUGH:

2 (.25 OUNCE) PACKAGES DRY YEAST	2 (7 G)
1 TEASPOON SUGAR	5 ML
2½ CUPS WARM WATER (110° F), DIVIDED	625 ML
1 (18 OUNCE) YELLOW CAKE MIX	1 (520 G)
4½ CUPS FLOUR, DIVIDED	1 L 125 ML

FILLING:

1 (8 OUNCE) PACKAGE CREAM CHEESE, SOFTENED	1 (228 G)
¼ CUP SUGAR	60 ML
1 EGG, SEPARATED	1
1 TABLESPOON SOUR CREAM	15 ML
½ TEASPOON VANILLA	2 ML
½ CUP RAISINS	125 ML
½ CUP GROUND WALNUTS	125 ML

TOPPING:

1 EGG WHITE	1
2 TABLESPOONS SUGAR	30 ML
¼ CUP CHOPPED WALNUTS	60 ML

◆ To prepare dough, stir yeast and sugar in small bowl with ½ cup (125 mL) water. Let sit for 10 minutes until foamy.

◆ In large bowl, combine cake mix and flour. Stir in water and yeast mixture plus remaining 2 cups (500 mL) water. Mix well.

◆ Cover and let rise in warm location until double in size (about 1 hour).

◆ To prepare the filling, cream the cheese and sugar until light and fluffy. Add egg yolk, sour cream and vanilla. Blend well. Stir in raisins and walnuts. Set aside.

(CONTINUED ON NEXT PAGE.)

(CONTINUED)

◆ Roll out dough on heavily floured surface into rectangle about 18 x 16 inches (45 x 40 cm). Spread filling evenly over dough.

◆ Roll dough jelly-roll fashion starting from longest side. Cut roll in half and place 2 rolls seam-side down on greased cookie sheet.

◆ Cut slashes 2 inches (5 cm) apart in tops of rolls. Cover loosely with plastic wrap and set aside to rise again until doubled in size.

◆ Preheat oven to 350° (176° C). Brush tops of rolls with egg white. Sprinkle 1 tablespoon (15 mL) sugar, then half the walnuts over each roll.

◆ Bake for 25 to 30 minutes until brown.

HELPING DOUGH RISE

To provide a good environment for rising dough and to hasten the process, you can use the following method. Take a small or medium pan of boiling water and place it on the bottom rack of your oven, then place the covered dough on the rack above.

The warmth from the hot water helps the dough rise, keeps the air around it moist and prevents it from drying out. (It also provides a place to stash the bowl out of sight and out of your way, so you can clean up the mess you made making it!)

STICKY BUNS

Try these for a brunch or morning get-together. Soft and fluffy, topped with caramel-coated pecans, they look and taste like they came straight from the bakery!

2 (.25 OUNCE) PACKAGES DRY YEAST	**2 (7 G)**
2 ½ CUPS WARM (110° F) (43° C) WATER	**625 ML**
1 (18 OUNCE) YELLOW CAKE MIX	**1 (520 G)**
4 CUPS FLOUR	**1 L**
½ CUP BUTTER, DIVIDED	**125 ML**
2 TABLESPOONS SUGAR	**30 ML**
1 TEASPOON CINNAMON	**5 ML**
¼ CUP LIGHT CORN SYRUP	**60 ML**
¼ CUP PACKED BROWN SUGAR	**60 ML**
2 CUPS PECAN HALVES	**500 ML**

◆ Dissolve yeast in water and let rest for 10 minutes. In large bowl, combine cake mix and flour. Stir in water and yeast mixture and blend well.

◆ Cover bowl and let rise in warm place until double in volume (about 1 hour).

◆ Roll dough on floured work surface into rectangle about a ¼ inch thick (about 12 x 24 inches in diameter). Melt ¼ cup (60 mL) butter and spread over dough using pastry brush or back of spoon.

◆ Combine sugar and cinnamon in small bowl, and sprinkle evenly over dough. Starting with longest side, roll dough into a log.

(CONTINUED ON NEXT PAGE.)

(CONTINUED)

◆ Combine corn syrup, brown sugar and remaining ¼ cup (60 mL) butter in small saucepan. Cook over low heat, stirring frequently, until butter melts and mixture is smooth.

◆ Pour evenly into bottom of well-greased 10 x 15-inch (25 x 38 cm) baking pan. Sprinkle pecans evenly over top.

◆ Slice dough into 1½ to 2-inch (3 to 5 cm) pieces and place close together (flat side down) over pecans in pan.

◆ Cover with plastic wrap and let rise again until double in size (about 30 minutes). Bake for 25 minutes or until cake tester inserted halfway comes out clean.

◆ Remove from oven, let rest for 2 to 3 minutes, then unmold onto serving tray. Cool slightly and serve warm or cold. (Makes about 20 rolls.)

CHOCOLATE-FILLED CUPCAKES

1 (18 OUNCE) DEVIL'S FOOD CAKE MIX	1 (520 G)
1 ⅓ CUPS BUTTERMILK	310 ML
4 EGGS, DIVIDED	4
⅓ CUP VEGETABLE OIL	80 ML
1 CUP MINIATURE SEMI-SWEET CHOCOLATE CHIPS, DIVIDED	250 ML
1 (8 OUNCE) PACKAGE CREAM CHEESE, SOFTENED	1 (228 G)
½ CUP SUGAR	125 ML

◆ Preheat oven to 350° (176° C). In large bowl, combine cake mix, buttermilk, 3 eggs and oil.

◆ Beat on low speed to blend, then beat on medium for 2 minutes. Stir ½ cup (125 mL) chocolate chips into batter and set aside.

◆ In medium bowl, beat cream cheese, sugar and remaining egg until mixture is smooth. Melt remaining ½ cup (125 mL) chocolate chips and add to cheese mixture. Beat until well blended.

◆ Prepare 24 muffin pans, by either greasing and flouring or using paper baking cups. Fill each cup half full with batter.

◆ Drop 1 tablespoon (15 mL) chocolate-cheese mixture in center and spoon remaining batter evenly. Bake for 25 minutes.

I love being able to use a cake mix to make the recipes in "Special Cakes" from page 118 to 127. Pastries of this sort always looked so complicated to me and I found myself hesitating before trying to make them. When I started making them with the cake mixes, I realized how easy they are!

Yes, they take a little longer than a cake, because once you mix the dough, you have to wait for it to rise, then work it, make your pastry and then let it rise again, but the whole process can be done within a couple of hours. And then you have hot, fresh baked goods that look like you went to the bakery.

Another great thing about using a mix is the flavor. The dough has a sweeter taste to it, which I like, and it's very moist. One of my biggest complaints about buying cinnamon rolls or pastry at the store is that it's so often a little dry— too "bready." These aren't!

These are great "Saturday morning" recipes. Try preparing as much as you can the night before, by getting out the non-perishable ingredients and utensils you'll need, then put it together first thing in the morning. (After you have had that first cup of coffee of course.)

CAKES & ICINGS:

MIX AND MATCH FLAVORS

	BOILED WHITE ICING, P. 83	BROILED COCONUT FROSTING, P. 25	BROWN SUGAR FROSTING, P. 88
AUTUMN-SPICE CAKE, P. 96		◆	◆
BANANA NUT CAKE, P. 29	◆	◆	◆
BLACK WALNUT CAKE, P. 99			◆
BLUEBERRY CREAM CHEESE CAKE, P. 63			
COCONUT CAKE, P. 73	◆		
COOL AND FRUITY LEMON CAKE, P. 22	◆	◆	
DATE-SPICE CAKE, P. 69			◆
DEVILS FOOD CREAM CHEESE CAKE, P. 97	◆		
HONEY-CITRUS CAKE, P. 34	◆	◆	
LEMON CREAM CHEESE SWIRL CAKE, P. 27	◆		
NEVER-ENDING CHOCOLATE BUNDT CAKE, P. 66	◆		
OATMEAL-SPICE CAKE, P. 88			◆
ORANGE-BANANA BUNDT CAKE, P. 80	◆		
WHITE CHOCOLATE BUNDT CAKE, P. 65	◆		

The possible combinations of cakes and icings are almost endless. So, we've listed only a few of the many flavor combinations that work well together in this handy table. When you're in the mood for a little variety, try some of the suggested pairings. Don't be limited by what you see here, however. Use your own creativity and likes to match other cake and icing combinations to suit your tastes!

BUTTER-PECAN FROSTING P. 91	CHOCOLATE-FUDGE ICING, P. 87	CREAM CHEESE ICING, P. 98	MAPLE FROSTING P. 99	WHIPPED TOPPING P. 23	WHITE FROSTING P. 95
◆		◆	◆		
◆		◆		◆	◆
			◆		
		◆		◆	◆
	◆	◆		◆	◆
		◆		◆	◆
			◆		
	◆	◆			◆
		◆		◆	◆
		◆		◆	◆
	◆	◆			◆
◆			◆		
	◆	◆		◆	◆
	◆				◆

Just Snap Your Fingers

You'll be amazed at the wide range of cookie styles and flavors you can create by using a cookie mix or cake mix as a base. For instance, the plain flavor of a sugar cookie mix provides a starting point for creating all kinds of great-tasting and great-looking cookies with the addition of a few simple ingredients. A cake mix can be used to create drop cookies or rolled cookies in less time than it would normally take to make a batch from scratch.

Thumbprint cookies, round cookies with a jam-filled center, look pretty and taste great. By adding a few ingredients to a humble sugar cookie dough, you can turn out a variety of tasty cookies in very little time.

Follow the basic thumbprint cookie recipe, using the ingredients specified in the variations that follow to create a range of colorful, attractive, delicious cookies.

To speed your cookie-making, prepare the cookie dough the day before (it takes about 5 minutes), then tightly cover and refrigerate it until you're ready to use it. You'll be far ahead of the game when you're ready to bake.

BASIC THUMBPRINT COOKIE RECIPE

1 (18 OUNCE) SUGAR COOKIE MIX	1 (520 G
½ CUP (1 STICK) BUTTER, MELTED	125 ML
1 EGG	1
⅓ CUP FLOUR	80 ML
1 EGG WHITE, OPTIONAL	1
1¼ TO 1½ CUPS CHOPPED NUTS OR	310 TO 375 ML
COCONUT OR ¼ CUP SUGAR	60 ML
⅓ TO ½ CUP JAM	80 TO 125 ML

◆ Preheat oven to 375° (190° C). In medium bowl, combine cookie mix, melted butter and egg. Gradually stir in flour until dough blends well.

◆ Take dough by teaspoonfuls and roll into balls between palms of your hands. Depending on recipe instructions, either roll each ball in sugar or dip in egg white and roll in ground nuts. (Egg white, chopped nuts, coconut or sugar may change according to variations on page 133.)

◆ Place 2 to 3 inches (5 to 7 cm) apart on ungreased cookie sheet and using blunt handle of spoon or your thumb to make slight depression in top of each cookie. (Make it about half the depth of the cookie.) Fill with ½ teaspoonful (.5 mL) jam.

◆ Bake for 10 to 13 minutes or until edges are light brown. Remove from oven and cool on cookie sheet for 1 minute, then transfer to cooling rack.

VARIATIONS FOR BASIC THUMBPRINT COOKIES

Recipe for Basic Thumbprint Cookies is on page 132.

CHERRY-ALMOND THUMBPRINT COOKIES
◆ Add 1 teaspoon (5 mL) almond extract to cookie mix with butter and egg. Dip balls in egg white and roll in finely chopped or ground almonds. Fill with cherry jam. (Makes about 2½ to 3 dozen.)

CHOCOLATE-RASPBERRY THUMBPRINT COOKIES
◆ Add ¼ (1 mL) teaspoon almond extract and 3 tablespoons (45 mL) unsweetened cocoa powder to the dough. Roll balls in sugar. Fill with raspberry jam. (Makes 2½ to 3 dozen.)

CINNAMON-ORANGE THUMBPRINT COOKIES
◆ Add 1 teaspoon (5 mL) cinnamon to cookie mix. Dip balls in egg white and roll in finely chopped or ground walnuts. Fill with orange marmalade. (Makes 3 to 3½ dozen.)

ISLAND-PINEAPPLE THUMBPRINT COOKIES
◆ Add 1 teaspoon (5 mL) lemon flavoring to cookie mix. Dip balls in egg white and roll in coconut. Fill with pineapple jam. (Makes 3 to 3½ dozen.)

PEANUT BUTTER & JELLY THUMBPRINT COOKIES
◆ Add ½ cup (125 mL) creamy peanut butter to dough before adding flour. Increase flour to ½ cup (125 mL). Roll in sugar. Fill with grape jam. (Makes 3½ to 4 dozen.)

(CONTINUED ON NEXT PAGE.)

(CONTINUED)

CHOCOLATE-CHERRY THUMBPRINT COOKIES

◆ Add 1 tablespoon (15 mL) cocoa powder to cookie mix. Stir in ½ cup (125 mL) miniature semi-sweet chocolate chips. Roll in sugar. Fill with cherry jam. (Makes about 3 dozen.)

SPICY MINCEMEAT THUMBPRINT COOKIES

◆ Add 1 teaspoon (5 mL) cinnamon to cookie mix. Dip balls in egg white and roll in finely chopped or ground walnuts. Fill with mincemeat. (Makes about 3 dozen.)

HOLIDAY FRUITCAKE THUMBPRINT COOKIES

◆ Add 1 teaspoon (5 mL) allspice and ½ cup (125 mL) fruitcake mix (or combination of finely chopped glaceed fruit). Roll in sugar. Fill with cherry jam.

APRICOT-ANISETTE THUMBPRINT COOKIES

◆ Add 1 teaspoon (5 mL) anise extract and 1 teaspoon (5 mL) lemon zest. Dip balls in egg white and roll in chopped almonds. Fill with apricot jam.

MALTED MILK BALL
CHOCOLATE CHIP COOKIES

1 (18 OUNCE) CHOCOLATE CHIP COOKIE MIX	1 (520 G)
½ CUP (1 STICK) BUTTER, SOFTENED	125 ML
1 EGG	1
1 CUP CRUSHED MALTED MILK BALLS	250 ML
½ CUP CHOPPED PECANS	125 ML

◆ Preheat oven to 350° (176° C). In medium bowl, combine cookie mix, butter and egg. Mix well.

◆ Stir in malted milk balls and pecans and blend well.

◆ Drop by heaping teaspoonfuls onto greased cookie sheet and bake for 12 to 15 minutes.

◆ Remove from oven, and let cookies cool on cookie sheet for 1 minute. Transfer to cooling rack. (Makes about 2½ to 3 dozen.)

CREAM CHEESE APRICOT COOKIES

4 OUNCES CREAM CHEESE, SOFTENED	**115 G**
¼ CUP (½ STICK) BUTTER, SOFTENED	**60 ML**
1 EGG	**1**
1 (18 OUNCE) SUGAR COOKIE MIX	**1 (520 G)**
½ CUP DRIED CHOPPED APRICOTS	**125 ML**

◆ Preheat oven to 375° (190° C). In medium bowl, cream cheese and butter until they blend well. Add egg and beat until smooth.

◆ Stir in cookie mix (mixture will be thick). Stir in apricots.

◆ Drop by rounded teaspoonfuls onto ungreased cookie sheet. Bake for 12 to 14 minutes or until edges are light brown.

◆ Remove from oven and cool on cookie sheet for 1 minute before transferring to cooling rack.

Because I really do not like the tedious job of chopping apricots, I like to use the Sunsweet brand "Fruitlings". These dried fruits are already cut in a size perfect for baking.

ORANGE-DATE WALNUT COOKIES

*These delightful cookies are crispy and
light with just a hint of cinnamon.*

1 (17 OUNCE) SUGAR COOKIE MIX	1 (520 G)
½ CUP (1 STICK) BUTTER, MELTED	125 ML
1 EGG	1
1 TEASPOON ORANGE EXTRACT	5 ML
½ TEASPOON CINNAMON	2 ML
½ CUP CHOPPED DATES	125 ML
½ CUP COARSELY CHOPPED WALNUTS	125 ML

◆ Preheat oven to 375° (190° C). Combine cookie mix, butter, egg, orange extract and cinnamon in medium bowl. Blend well.

◆ Stir in dates and walnuts.

◆ Drop by heaping teaspoonfuls onto ungreased cookie sheet. Bake for 9 to 10 minutes or until light brown around edges.

◆ Remove cookies from oven and cool on cookie sheet for 1 minute before transferring to cooling rack.

MOLASSES-SPICE COOKIES

1 (17 OUNCE) SUGAR COOKIE MIX	1 (520 G)
½ TEASPOON GROUND GINGER	2 ML
¼ TEASPOON NUTMEG	1 ML
1 TEASPOON CINNAMON	5 ML
PINCH GROUND CLOVES	
2 EGGS	2
½ CUP (1 STICK) BUTTER, MELTED	125 ML
¼ CUP MOLASSES	60 ML
½ CUP RAISINS, OPTIONAL	125 ML

◆ Preheat oven to 375° (190° C). In large bowl, combine cookie mix, ginger, nutmeg, cinnamon and cloves. Stir thoroughly to mix.

◆ Add eggs, butter and molasses and mix well. If desired, stir in raisins.

◆ Drop by rounded teaspoonfuls onto well greased cookie sheet. Bake for 7 to 9 minutes or until light brown around edges.

◆ Cool cookies on cookie sheet for 1 minute and transfer to cooling rack. (Makes 2 to 3 dozen.)

TRAIL MIX COOKIES

1 (17 OUNCE) OATMEAL COOKIE MIX	1 (520 G)
3 TABLESPOONS WATER	45 ML
⅓ CUP VEGETABLE OIL	80 ML
1 EGG	1
1 CUP (6 OUNCES) TRAIL MIX (CHOCOLATE CANDY, RAISINS, CASHEWS AND ALMONDS)	250 ML

◆ Preheat oven to 350° (176° C). In medium bowl, combine cookie mix, water, oil and egg and mix well.

◆ Stir in trail mix.

◆ Drop by heaping teaspoonfuls onto ungreased cookie sheet.

◆ Bake for 10 to 12 minutes or until edges are light brown. Remove from oven and cool on cookie sheet for 1 minute. Transfer to cooling rack. (Makes 2 to 2½ dozen.)

WHITE CHOCOLATE MACADAMIA NUT COOKIES

1 (18 OUNCE) WHITE CAKE MIX WITH PUDDING	1 (520 G)
½ CUP (1 STICK) BUTTER	125 ML
2 EGGS	2
1 CUP WHITE CHOCOLATE BAKING CHIPS	250 ML
¾ CUP COARSELY CHOPPED MACADAMIA NUTS, TOASTED	180 ML

◆ Preheat oven to 350° (176° C). In medium bowl, combine cake mix, butter and eggs. Beat on medium speed until well blended. Stir in white chocolate chips and nuts.

◆ Drop by rounded teaspoonfuls onto ungreased cookie sheet. Bake for 10 to 12 minutes. Cool cookies for 1 minute on baking sheet and transfer to wire rack. (Makes about 3 dozen.)

Learn how to toast pecans on page 91.

COCONUT MACAROONS

1 (18 OUNCE) FRENCH VANILLA CAKE MIX OR WHITE CAKE MIX WITH PUDDING	1 (520 G)
½ CUP (1 STICK) BUTTER	125 ML
3 EGGS	3
1 TEASPOON VANILLA	5 ML
½ CUP SUGAR	125 ML
3 CUPS SHREDDED COCONUT	750 ML

◆ Preheat oven to 350° (176° C). In large bowl, combine cake mix, butter, eggs, vanilla and sugar. Beat on medium speed until well blended.

◆ Stir in coconut. Drop by rounded teaspoonfuls onto ungreased cookie sheet.

◆ Bake for 10 to 12 minutes. Cool cookies on cookie sheet for 1 minute and transfer to wire cooling rack. (Makes approximately 3 dozen.)

MINT-CHOCOLATE COOKIES

1 (18 OUNCE) SWISS CHOCOLATE CAKE MIX	1 (520 G)
1 EGG	1
4 OUNCES FROZEN WHIPPED TOPPING, THAWED	115 G
¼ TEASPOON PEPPERMINT EXTRACT	1 ML
POWDERED SUGAR	

◆ Preheat oven to 350° (176° C). In large bowl, combine cake mix, egg, whipped topping and peppermint extract.

◆ Blend on low speed until thoroughly mixed.

◆ Take heaping teaspoonfuls of dough and roll into balls, then roll in powdered sugar. Place 3 inches apart on greased cookie sheet and bake for 10 to 12 minutes.

CHOCOLATEY CHOCOLATE CHIP OATMEAL COOKIES

½ CUP (1 STICK) BUTTER, SOFTENED	125 ML
2 EGGS	2
1 (18 OUNCE) GERMAN CHOCOLATE CAKE MIX	1 (520 G)
¾ CUP OLD-FASHION OATS	180 ML
¾ CUP SEMI-SWEET CHOCOLATE CHIPS	180 ML
½ CUP COARSELY CHOPPED PECANS	125 ML

◆ Preheat oven to 375° (190° C). In large bowl, blend butter with eggs. Stir in cake mix and oats. Blend well.

◆ Stir in chocolate chips and pecans. Drop by heaping teaspoonfuls onto greased cookie sheet.

◆ Bake for 10 to 12 minutes (until edges are slightly brown). Remove from oven and cool on cookie sheet for 1 minute. Remove cookies to cooling rack.

ORANGE-PECAN COOKIES

1 (18 OUNCE) SUGAR COOKIE MIX	1 (520 G)
½ CUP (1 STICK) BUTTER, MELTED	125 ML
1 EGG	1
1 TEASPOON ORANGE EXTRACT	5 ML
½ CUP CHOPPED PECANS	125 ML

◆ Preheat oven to 350° (176° C). In medium bowl, combine cookie mix, butter, egg, orange extract and pecans. Mix well.

◆ Drop by heaping teaspoonsful onto ungreased cookie sheet. Bake for 12 to 13 minutes or until light brown around edges.

◆ Remove from oven and cool on cookie sheet for 1 minute. Transfer cookies to cooling rack. (Makes 2 to 2½ dozen.)

NO-BAKE BUTTERSCOTCH COOKIES

More like a candy than a cookie,
these little butterscotch treats are delightful.

2 CUPS SUGAR	500 ML
¾ CUP (1 ½ STICKS) BUTTER	180 ML
⅔ CUP EVAPORATED MILK	160 ML
1 (3 OUNCE) PACKAGE BUTTERSCOTCH	
INSTANT PUDDING MIX	1 (85 G)
3 ½ CUPS OLD-FASHION OATS	875 ML
¾ CUP BUTTERSCOTCH BAKING CHIPS	180 ML
½ CUP CHOPPED PECANS	125 ML

◆ In medium saucepan, bring sugar, butter and evaporated milk to a boil, stirring constantly. Boil for 1 minute, then remove from heat.

◆ Stir in pudding mix, then oats and mix well. Cool for 10 minutes, then stir in butterscotch chips and pecans. (Note: Butterscotch chips will melt, so stir until mixture is smooth.)

◆ Drop by heaping teaspoonfuls onto wax paper to harden. (Makes 3 to 4 dozen.)

VARIATION FOR CHOCOLATE LOVERS:
Substitute chocolate fudge pudding mix for the butterscotch and omit butterscotch chips.

CHOCOLATEY CHOCOLATE CHIP OATMEAL COOKIES

½ CUP (1 STICK) BUTTER, SOFTENED	125 ML
2 EGGS	2
1 (18 OUNCE) GERMAN CHOCOLATE CAKE MIX	1 (520 G)
¾ CUP OLD-FASHION OATS	180 ML
¾ CUP SEMI-SWEET CHOCOLATE CHIPS	180 ML
½ CUP COARSELY CHOPPED PECANS	125 ML

◆ Preheat oven to 375° (190° C). In large bowl, blend butter with eggs. Stir in cake mix and oats. Blend well.

◆ Stir in chocolate chips and pecans. Drop by heaping teaspoonfuls onto greased cookie sheet.

◆ Bake for 10 to 12 minutes (until edges are slightly brown). Remove from oven and cool on cookie sheet for 1 minute. Remove cookies to cooling rack.

ORANGE-PECAN COOKIES

1 (18 OUNCE) SUGAR COOKIE MIX	1 (520 G)
½ CUP (1 STICK) BUTTER, MELTED	125 ML
1 EGG	1
1 TEASPOON ORANGE EXTRACT	5 ML
½ CUP CHOPPED PECANS	125 ML

◆ Preheat oven to 350° (176° C). In medium bowl, combine cookie mix, butter, egg, orange extract and pecans. Mix well.

◆ Drop by heaping teaspoonsful onto ungreased cookie sheet. Bake for 12 to 13 minutes or until light brown around edges.

◆ Remove from oven and cool on cookie sheet for 1 minute. Transfer cookies to cooling rack. (Makes 2 to 2½ dozen.)

NO-BAKE BUTTERSCOTCH COOKIES

More like a candy than a cookie,
these little butterscotch treats are delightful.

2 CUPS SUGAR	**500 ML**
¾ CUP (1½ STICKS) BUTTER	**180 ML**
⅔ CUP EVAPORATED MILK	**160 ML**
1 (3 OUNCE) PACKAGE BUTTERSCOTCH	
INSTANT PUDDING MIX	**1 (85 G)**
3½ CUPS OLD-FASHION OATS	**875 ML**
¾ CUP BUTTERSCOTCH BAKING CHIPS	**180 ML**
½ CUP CHOPPED PECANS	**125 ML**

◆ In medium saucepan, bring sugar, butter and evaporated milk to a boil, stirring constantly. Boil for 1 minute, then remove from heat.

◆ Stir in pudding mix, then oats and mix well. Cool for 10 minutes, then stir in butterscotch chips and pecans. (Note: Butterscotch chips will melt, so stir until mixture is smooth.)

◆ Drop by heaping teaspoonfuls onto wax paper to harden. (Makes 3 to 4 dozen.)

VARIATION FOR CHOCOLATE LOVERS:
Substitute chocolate fudge pudding mix for the butterscotch and omit butterscotch chips.

SPICY OATMEAL COOKIES

¼ CUP PACKED BROWN SUGAR	60 ML
¼ CUP SUGAR	60 ML
¾ CUP FLOUR	180 ML
½ TEASPOON BAKING SODA	2 ML
PINCH SALT	
5 (2 OUNCE) RAISINS AND SPICE INSTANT OATMEAL PACKETS	5 (57 G)
½ CUP (1 STICK) BUTTER, SOFTENED	125 ML
1 EGG	1
½ TEASPOON VANILLA	2 ML

◆ Preheat oven to 350° (176° C). In large bowl, combine sugars, flour, baking soda, salt and oatmeal.

◆ In small bowl, combine butter, egg and vanilla and mix well. Add to dry ingredients and blend thoroughly.

◆ Drop by heaping teaspoonfuls onto ungreased cookie sheet and bake for 12 to 14 minutes until nicely brown.

◆ Cool on cookie sheet for 1 minute and transfer to wire rack. (Makes 1½ to 2 dozen.)

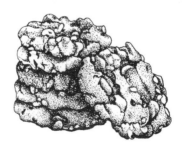

MOCHA-CINNAMON SNAPS

For an extra special finishing touch, I usually press a whole pecan lightly into the surface of each dough ball before baking. With the chocolate drizzled over, these cookies look like little gourmet treats—no one would ever guess how fast and easy they are to make.

1 (17 OUNCE) SUGAR COOKIE MIX	1 (487 G)
2 TABLESPOONS UNSWEETENED COCOA	30 ML
2 TEASPOONS CINNAMON	10 ML
1 TEASPOON INSTANT COFFEE GRANULES	5 ML
½ CUP (1 STICK) BUTTER, MELTED	125 ML
1 EGG	1

◆ Preheat oven to 375° (190° C). In medium bowl, combine cookie mix, cocoa, cinnamon and coffee. Mix well.

◆ Add butter and egg and mix dough thoroughly.

◆ Drop by rounded teaspoonfuls onto ungreased cookie sheet. Bake for 10 minutes.

◆ Cool on cookie sheet for 1 minute and transfer to cooling rack.

◆ When cool, drizzle *Chocolate Glaze* on next page over cookies. (Use a zig-zag motion to make lines of chocolate across cookie surface.) Makes 3 dozen.

(CONTINUED ON NEXT PAGE.)

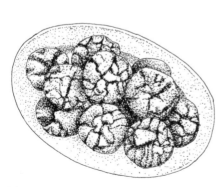

(CONTINUED)

CHOCOLATE GLAZE:

½ **CUP MILK CHOCOLATE OR**	
SEMI-SWEET CHOCOLATE CHIPS	**125 ML**
1 TEASPOON SHORTENING	**5 ML**

◆ In small saucepan, combine chocolate and shortening. Cook over low heat, stirring constantly, until chocolate melts. (Or, place chocolate and shortening in small microwave-safe bowl, cook on low power for 2 to 4 minutes and stop after each minute to stir.)

◆ Make drizzling easier by placing melted chocolate mixture in a plastic bag (like a sandwich bag), twist bag above chocolate and snip a tiny piece of the corner. Squeeze gently to dispense glaze.

If you're in a hurry, dropping these cookies by teaspoonful does the trick—but to make a really pretty, perfectly symmetrical cookie, take the teaspoonful of dough and roll it into a ball before placing it on the cookie sheet. As the cookie bakes, it will become round and smooth.

ICED-LEMON POPPY SEED COOKIES

These cookies are "cake-like" and very light.
They mound slightly when they bake.

1 (18 OUNCE) LEMON CAKE MIX	1 (520 G)
1 (8 OUNCE) CONTAINER SOUR CREAM	1 (228 G)
1 EGG	1
2 TABLESPOONS BUTTER, SOFTENED	30 ML
3 TABLESPOONS POPPY SEEDS	45 ML
¼ TEASPOON ALMOND EXTRACT	2 ML

◆ Preheat oven to 350° (176° C). In large bowl, combine cake mix, sour cream, egg, butter, poppy seeds and almond extract. Mix well by hand or with electric mixer on low speed until well blended.

◆ Drop by rounded teaspoonsful 2 inches (5 cm) apart onto greased cookie sheets.

◆ Bake for 11 to 13 minutes or until golden brown. Cool for 1 minute on cookie sheets and transfer to cooling rack. (Makes 2½ to 3 dozen.)

◆ When cool, drizzle *Powdered Sugar Glaze* over top.

POWDERED SUGAR GLAZE:	
1 TABLESPOON PLUS 1 TEASPOON MILK	15 ML
¼ TEASPOON ALMOND EXTRACT	2 ML
1 CUP POWDERED SUGAR	250 ML

◆ In small bowl, stir milk and almond extract into powdered sugar until mixture is smooth. Drizzle over cookies in a zig-zag fashion.

To drizzle glaze over cookies, I put it in a plastic
bag (like a sandwich bag) and snip a tiny piece
off the corner. I then twist the top of the bag above
the icing and squeeze lightly to dispense it.

DOUBLE CHOCOLATE CHIP COOKIES

1 (18 OUNCE) CHOCOLATE CAKE MIX WITH PUDDING	**1 (520 G)**
½ CUP (1 STICK) BUTTER	**125 ML**
1 TEASPOON VANILLA	**5 ML**
2 EGGS	**2**
1 CUP SEMI-SWEET CHOCOLATE CHIPS	**250 ML**
¾ CUP CHOPPED PECANS	**180 ML**

◆ Preheat oven to 350° (176° C). In medium bowl, combine cake mix, butter, vanilla and eggs. Beat on medium speed until well blended.

◆ Stir in chocolate chips and pecans.

◆ Drop by rounded teaspoonfuls onto ungreased cookie sheet and bake for 10 to 12 minutes.

◆ Cool for 1 minute on cookie sheet and remove to wire rack. (Makes about 3 dozen.)

BLACK FOREST CHERRY COOKIES

These cookies look and taste great even without the frosting.

1 (17 OUNCE) SUGAR COOKIE MIX	1 (487 G)
½ CUP (1 STICK) BUTTER, MELTED	125 ML
1 EGG	1
½ CUP MINIATURE SEMI-SWEET CHOCOLATE CHIPS	125 ML
½ CUP QUARTERED MARASCHINO CHERRIES	
WITH JUICE	125 ML

◆ Preheat oven to 375° (190° C). In medium bowl, combine cookie mix, butter and egg. Mix well.

◆ Stir in chocolate chips and maraschino cherries.

◆ Drop by rounded teaspoonfuls onto ungreased cookie sheet. Bake for 9 to 10 minutes or until edges are light brown.

◆ Cool cookies on cookie sheets for 1 minute before transferring to cooling rack.

◆ When cool, frost with *Chocolate Frosting* on next page, if desired.

(CONTINUED ON NEXT PAGE.)

(CONTINUED)

CHOCOLATE FROSTING:

3 (1 OUNCE) SQUARES SEMI-SWEET CHOCOLATE	3 (28 G)
2 TABLESPOONS BUTTER	30 ML
2 CUPS POWDERED SUGAR	500 ML
2 TABLESPOONS HALF-AND-HALF OR MILK	30 ML
1 TO 2 TABLESPOONS	
MARASCHINO CHERRY SYRUP	15 TO 30 ML

◆ Combine chocolate and butter in small saucepan. Cook over low heat, stirring constantly, until chocolate melts. Remove from heat and let cool slightly.

◆ In medium bowl, combine chocolate mixture with ½ cup (125 mL) powdered sugar and mix well.

◆ Add half-and-half and cherry syrup (start with 1 tablespoon (15 mL) and add a little more syrup if needed) and beat until mixture is smooth.

◆ Gradually add remaining powdered sugar, beating after each addition until mixture is smooth and reaches frosting consistency.

OATMEAL-ORANGE DATE COOKIES

1 (18 OUNCE) OATMEAL COOKIE MIX	1 (520 G)
½ CUP FLOUR	125 ML
⅓ CUP BUTTER, MELTED	80 ML
1 EGG	1
¾ CUP MARMALADE	180 ML
½ CUP CHOPPED DATES	125 ML
¾ CUP SHREDDED COCONUT	180 ML
¾ CUP CHOPPED WALNUTS	180 ML

◆ Preheat oven to 375° (190° C). In medium bowl, combine cookie mix and flour. Add butter, egg and marmalade and mix well to blend.

◆ Stir in dates, coconut and walnuts.

◆ Drop by heaping teaspoonfuls onto greased cookie sheet. Bake for 10 to 12 minutes. Let cookies cool on baking sheet for 1 minute before transferring to cooling rack. (Makes 3 dozen.)

OATMEAL-RAISIN COOKIES

1 (18 OUNCE) SPICE CAKE MIX	1 (520 G)
1 CUP QUICK-COOKING OATS	250 ML
1 CUP (2 STICKS) BUTTER, MELTED	250 ML
1 EGG	1
½ CUP MILK	125 ML
1 TEASPOON VANILLA	5 ML
¾ CUP CHOPPED WALNUTS	180 ML
1 CUP RAISINS	250 ML

◆ Preheat oven to 350° (176° C). In large bowl, beat cake mix, oats, butter, egg, milk and vanilla until thoroughly blended. Mix in walnuts and raisins.

◆ Drop by rounded teaspoonfuls onto ungreased cookie sheet and bake for 9 to 11 minutes. Cool on cookie sheet for 1 minute and transfer to cooling rack.

BANANA-BUTTER PECAN COOKIES

1 (17 OUNCE) OATMEAL COOKIE MIX	**1 (487 G)**
1 EGG	**1**
5 TABLESPOONS BUTTER, MELTED	**75 ML**
¾ CUP MASHED BANANAS	**180 ML**
¾ CUP CHOPPED PECANS	**180 ML**

◆ Preheat oven to 375° (190° C). In large bowl, combine cookie mix with egg, butter and bananas. Mix well.

◆ Stir in chopped pecans until well blended.

◆ Drop by heaping teaspoonfuls onto lightly greased cookie sheet and bake for 9 to 10 minutes or until light brown around edges.

◆ Cool on cookie sheet for 1 minute and transfer to cooling rack. (Makes 2½ to 3 dozen.)

MAPLE-ICED WALNUT COOKIES

1 (18 OUNCE) WHITE CAKE MIX	1 (520 G)
⅓ CUP MILK	80 ML
4 TABLESPOONS (½ STICK) BUTTER	60 ML
1 EGG	1
½ CUP PACKED BROWN SUGAR	125 ML
1½ CUPS COARSELY CHOPPED WALNUTS	375 ML

◆ Preheat oven to 350° (176° C). In large bowl, combine cake mix, milk, butter, egg and brown sugar. Beat on low speed until well blended, about 2 minutes.

◆ Stir in walnuts and drop by rounded teaspoonfuls onto lightly greased cookie sheet. Bake for 11 to 13 minutes until light brown.

◆ Remove from oven and cool for 1 minute, then transfer to cooling rack. When cool, frost with *Maple Icing*.

MAPLE ICING:

1½ CUPS POWDERED SUGAR	375 ML
3 TABLESPOONS BUTTER, SOFTENED	45 ML
¼ CUP MAPLE SYRUP	60 ML

◆ In medium bowl, cream some powdered sugar (about ½ cup) with butter and maple syrup until smooth.

◆ Add remaining powdered sugar ½ cup (125 mL) at a time, beating after each addition, until frosting reaches spreading consistency.

CHOCOLATE PINWHEELS

1 (17 OUNCE) SUGAR COOKIE MIX	**1 (487 G)**
⅓ CUP FLOUR	**80 ML**
½ CUP (1 STICK) BUTTER, MELTED	**125 ML**
1 EGG	**1**
1 (1 OUNCE) SQUARE SEMI-SWEET BAKING	
CHOCOLATE, MELTED	**1 (28 G)**

◆ Preheat oven to 375° (190° C). In medium bowl, combine cookie mix, flour, butter and egg. Mix thoroughly.

◆ Divide dough in half. To one half, add melted chocolate and mix until completely blended. (Refrigerate dough until chilled, if possible, to make it easier to work with.)

◆ On well floured surface, roll out white dough into a rectangle about ¼ inch thick. On another floured surface, roll out chocolate dough to same dimensions.

◆ Carefully lift chocolate dough and place over white dough. Roll from longest side jelly-roll fashion.

◆ Slice dough roll into pieces ¼ inch thick and place 3 inches apart on greased cookie sheet.

◆ Bake for about 10 minutes or until edges are light brown. Remove from oven and place on cooling rack. (Makes 2 to 3 dozen.)

153

DATE-NUT PINWHEEL COOKIES

1 CUP FINELY CHOPPED DATES	**250 ML**
½ CUP SUGAR	**125 ML**
½ CUP WATER	**125 ML**
½ CUP CHOPPED WALNUTS	**125 ML**
1 (17 OUNCE) SUGAR COOKIE MIX	**1 (487 G)**
¼ CUP FLOUR	**60 ML**

◆ In small saucepan, combine dates, sugar and water. Bring to a simmer and cook for 3 minutes on medium heat until thick. Remove from heat and cool. Set aside.

◆ Prepare cookie mix according to package directions and add flour so that it will roll out more easily. Divide dough in half and roll out one half into rectangle ¼ inch thick.

◆ Spread half filling mixture evenly over rolled out cookie dough. Sprinkle nuts evenly over mixture. Starting from long end, roll dough in jelly-roll fashion.

◆ Wrap in plastic wrap and refrigerate until firm. Repeat with remaining dough and filling mixture.

(CONTINUED ON NEXT PAGE.)

(CONTINUED)

◆ Preheat oven to 400° (204° C). Cut rolls into slices ¼ inch thick and place 2 inches apart on lightly greased baking sheet.

◆ Bake for 10 to 12 minutes or until light brown. Remove from oven and place on cooling rack.

HOLIDAY CREME-FILLED SANDWICH COOKIES

It's always fun to have baked goods that reflect the holiday spirit. The cookies that follow are all created from one simple sandwich cookie recipe: a plain sugar cookie colored, sometimes flavored and combined with a complementary filling. Simply follow the instructions for the basic dough and filling recipes below and modify them as outlined in the variations that follow.

BASIC DOUGH RECIPE:

1 (17 OUNCE) SUGAR COOKIE MIX	1 (487 G)
½ CUP (1 STICK) BUTTER, MELTED	125 ML
1 EGG	1

◆ In medium bowl, blend sugar cookie mix with butter and egg. Mix well.

◆ Preheat oven to 375° (190° C). Roll dough into balls 1 inch (2.5 cm) in diameter.

◆ Be sure and make each ball the same size, so that your cookies will be even when you put them together. Also be sure that you make an even amount of cookies, so that you'll have complete sandwiches.

(CONTINUED ON NEXT PAGE.)

(CONTINUED)

◆ Place 2 inches (5 cm) apart on ungreased cookie sheet. Bake for 8 to 10 minutes. (Try not to let edges get brown; if they do, reduce the baking time slightly.)

◆ Cool cookies on cookie sheet for 1 minute, then transfer onto cooling rack. When cool, place approximately 1 teaspoon filling in center back of 1 cookie.

◆ Place another cookie on top (flat side over filling) and use even pressure to press down in middle of top cookie to force filling outward to cookie edges.

BASIC CREME FILLING:
6 TABLESPOONS BUTTER, SOFTENED	**90 ML**
½ TEASPOON FLAVORING	**2 ML**
1 ½ CUPS POWDERED SUGAR	**375 ML**
1 TO 1 ½ TABLESPOONS	
HALF-AND-HALF OR MILK	**15 TO 22 ML**

◆ In medium bowl, cream butter, flavoring and half of powdered sugar. (Use flavoring listed with variations on pages 158 - 159.)

◆ Add 1 tablespoon (5 mL) half-and-half and beat well.

◆ Add remaining powdered sugar and enough half-and-half to make filling easy to work with, but not too thin.

(CONTINUED ON NEXT PAGE.)

VARIATIONS FOR SANDWICH COOKIES

Use these recipes with Basic Dough and Basic Filling
on pages 156 - 157.

#1. HALLOWEEN ORANGE-CHOCOLATE COOKIES

◆ Make sugar cookie dough (page 156) and add
½ teaspoon (2 mL) orange extract with butter and egg.
Add 4 drops red food coloring and 8 drops yellow to
make dough orange.

◆ Add 3 tablespoons (45 mL) cocoa powder to filling
(page 157).

VARIATION:

You can also make the reverse of the cookies above by
making the cookies chocolate and the filling orange.
Add 2 tablespoons (30 mL) cocoa powder to sugar
cookie mix, before adding butter and egg.

◆ To make orange-colored filling, add 2 drops red food
coloring and 4 drops yellow. If desired, add ¼ teaspoon
(2 mL) orange extract to flavor filling.

*(I actually like to make a batch of each
and mix them on a serving tray.)*

#2. PEPPERMINT-CHRISTMAS COOKIES

◆ Make sugar cookie dough (page 156). Divide dough in
half. Add 10 drops red food coloring to one half dough.

◆ Mix well so dough is evenly colored. Add 10 drops
green to other half and mix well.

(CONTINUED ON NEXT PAGE.)

(CONTINUED)

◆ Add ½ teaspoon (2 mL) peppermint extract to filling (page 156).

◆ To make cookies, place 1 green and 1 red cookie together with filling in the middle.

#3. VALENTINE'S DAY CHEERY-CHERRY COOKIES

◆ Make sugar cookie dough (page 156). Add 10 drops red food coloring to dough, but mix dough only enough to get a marbled effect, not to evenly color it.

◆ Add ⅓ cup (80 mL) minced maraschino cherries and ½ teaspoon (2 mL) clear vanilla flavoring to filling (page 156).

#4. PRETTY PASTEL EASTER COOKIES

◆ Make sugar cookie dough (page 156). Divide into thirds. Color one third peach by adding 1 drop red food coloring and 3 drops yellow.

◆ Color another one third purple by adding 3 drops blue food coloring and 3 drops red. Color remaining one third light green by adding 3 drops green food coloring.

◆ To filling (page 157) add ½ teaspoon (2 mL) lemon extract.

GINGER-JAM SANDWICH COOKIES

These cookies make a really fast, tasty treat to take to a
luncheon or other get-together. They're really pretty just
the way they are after you put them together, but look
extra special with a little powdered sugar sifted on top.

1 (17 OUNCE) SUGAR COOKIE MIX	1 (487 G)
2 TEASPOONS POWDERED GINGER	10 ML
½ TEASPOON CINNAMON	2 ML
¼ TEASPOON GROUND CLOVES	2 ML
½ CUP (1 STICK) BUTTER, MELTED	125 ML
1 EGG	1
½ CUP STRAWBERRY JAM	125 ML

◆ Preheat oven to 375° (190° C). In medium bowl, combine cookie mix with ginger, cinnamon and cloves. Stir well to blend. Add butter and egg and mix thoroughly.

◆ Take small pieces of dough and roll into balls about ¾ inch to 1 inch in diameter.

◆ Place 2 to 3 inches apart on ungreased cookie sheet and bake for 9 to 10 minutes. Transfer cookies to cooling rack.

◆ When completely cool, place ½ teaspoonful (.5 mL) jam in center of flat side of 1 cookie and top with flat side of another cookie. Press lightly to distribute jam to edges. (Makes 2½ to 3 dozen.)

GINGERBREAD-ROLLED COOKIES

*These cookies are great! They're a fast way to make
a delicious rolled cookie. When you're swamped at
Christmastime with the hustle and bustle of the
holiday season, you'll find these are a great way to enjoy
making holiday cookies without spending a lot of
time mixing the dough. There's less to clean up too!*

¾ CUP (1 ½ STICKS) BUTTER, SOFTENED	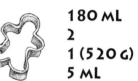	180 ML
2 EGG YOLKS		2
1 (18 OUNCE) SPICE CAKE MIX		1 (520 G)
1 TEASPOON GINGER		5 ML

◆ Preheat oven to 375° (190° C). In large bowl, combine butter and egg yolks. Gradually blend in cake mix and ginger. Mix well.

◆ Roll dough out to ⅛-inch thickness on lightly floured surface. Cut shapes with cookie cutter and place 2 inches (5 cm) apart on ungreased cookie sheets.

◆ Bake for 7 to 9 minutes or until edges are light brown. Remove from oven and cool cookies for 1 minute on cookie sheets before transferring to cooling rack.

*In order to roll the dough more easily and prevent
it from sticking to the rolling pin, I place a piece
of wax paper over the dough first and roll over it;
then I peel it away and cut out the cookies.*

*Also, to keep the cookies from stretching out of shape
when I pick them up, I slide a thin spatula (or turner)
under them and lift them onto the cookie sheet.*

CHOCOLATE-TURTLE COOKIES

This cookie version of the classic candy looks and tastes as good as it sounds. The turtle shapes are so easy (and cute!). Because you start with a cake mix, you can have the first batch of cookies out of the oven in no time.

1 (18 OUNCE) GERMAN CHOCOLATE OR DEVIL'S FOOD CAKE MIX WITH PUDDING	1 (520 ML)
½ CUP (1 STICK) BUTTER, SOFTENED	125 ML
1 TEASPOON VANILLA	5 ML
2 EGGS	2
4 TO 5 CUPS PECAN HALVES	1 TO 1 L 125 ML

◆ Preheat oven to 350° (176° C). In medium bowl, combine cake mix, butter, vanilla and eggs; beat on medium speed until well blended.

◆ Drop by small rounded teaspoonfuls onto greased cookie sheet, leaving enough room to add pecans to edges without crowding cookies.

◆ For each cookie, arrange 5 pecan halves in star shape around dough—1 for the head and 4 for legs—let pecans just butt up against the dough. As cookies bake they will flatten and expand to partially cover pecans.

◆ Bake for 12 to 15 minutes. Remove from oven and cool for 2 minutes on cookie sheet before removing to cooling rack.

◆ Cool slightly and top with *Caramel Topping* on next page.

(CONTINUED ON NEXT PAGE.)

(CONTINUED)

CARAMEL TOPPING:

1 (14 OUNCE) BAG (ABOUT 44) INDIVIDUALLY-WRAPPED CARAMEL CANDIES, UNWRAPPED	1 (420 G)
2 TABLESPOONS HALF-AND-HALF OR MILK	30 ML
2 TABLESPOONS BUTTER	30 ML

◆ In top of double boiler over boiling water, combine caramels, half-and-half and butter. Cook, stirring frequently, until caramels melt.

◆ Remove from heat, but keep double boiler intact, so caramel remains soft as you frost cookies.

◆ Place small spoonful caramel in center of cookie and smooth to edges of cookie with butter knife or spatula.

◆ Save some time by making caramel topping while first batch of cookies bakes. It can remain warm in double boiler and be ready for first batch of cookies after they've cooled for a couple of minutes.

Tip: Be sure to pick the nicest, plumpest pecans for these. (Note: I have tried making these with a cake mix that didn't contain pudding and they didn't come out as nicely. They were too thin.)

ORANGE-CHOCOLATE FILLED COOKIES

1 (18 OUNCE) BUTTER RECIPE YELLOW CAKE MIX	**1 (520 G)**
2 EGG YOLKS	**2**
2 TEASPOONS ORANGE EXTRACT	**10 ML**
¾ CUP (1 ½ STICKS) BUTTER, SOFTENED	**180 ML**
½ CUP MINIATURE SEMI-SWEET	
** CHOCOLATE CHIPS**	**125 ML**
½ CUP CHOPPED WALNUTS	**125 ML**

◆ Preheat oven to 375° (190° C). In large bowl, combine cake mix, egg yolks, orange extract and butter. Blend until thoroughly mixed.

◆ To prepare filling combine chocolate chips and walnuts in blender or food processor. Blend for about 30 seconds or until mixture starts to hold together.

◆ Divide dough in half and work with one half at a time. (Refrigerate unused dough until ready to use.)

◆ Roll dough out on well floured surface to ⅛ inch thickness. Cut 2½ inches (6 cm) diameter circles using biscuit cutter or round cookie cutter.

◆ Place 1 teaspoon (5 mL) filling mixture in center of 1 circle, gently spread it out, but do not extend it to edge. Place another cut out circle on top and use very thin spatula (or turner) to lift entire cookie to place it on cookie sheet.

◆ Crimp the edges gently with fork to seal. Repeat and allow 3 inches (7.6 cm) between cookies on baking sheet.

(CONTINUED ON NEXT PAGE.)

(CONTINUED)

◆ Bake cookies for 10 to 12 minutes or until light brown around edges.

◆ Remove from oven and cool cookies on cookie sheet for 1 minute before transferring to cooling rack.

◆ When cool, glaze with *Semi-Sweet Chocolate Glaze*. (I use a small plastic bag, like a sandwich bag and fill it with chocolate mixture, twist it above mixture, snip corner and squeeze gently to dispense the glaze.)

SEMI-SWEET CHOCOLATE GLAZE:
½ CUP SEMI-SWEET CHOCOLATE CHIPS   **125 ML**
1 TEASPOON SHORTENING   **5 ML**

◆ Melt chocolate and shortening in small saucepan over low heat, stirring constantly. Drizzle over cookies.

SPICY CINNAMON TWISTS

1 (17 OUNCE) SUGAR COOKIE MIX	1 (487 G)
½ CUP FLOUR	125 ML
½ CUP (1 STICK) BUTTER, MELTED	125 ML
1 EGG	1
1 TEASPOON MAPLE FLAVORING	5 ML
1 TEASPOON ALLSPICE	5 ML
1 TEASPOON GINGER	5 ML
¼ CUP SUGAR	60 ML
1 TEASPOON CINNAMON	5 ML

◆ Preheat oven to 375° (190° C). In medium bowl, combine cookie mix, flour, butter, egg, maple flavoring, allspice and ginger. Mix well.

◆ In small bowl, mix sugar and cinnamon. Pour into plate or shallow bowl. Set aside.

◆ Roll heaping tablespoons dough into ropes 6 inches (15 cm) long. Gently lift, fold in half (keeping loose ends even) and twist 3 times. Place on ungreased cookie sheet about 2 inches (5 cm) apart.

◆ Bake for 12 minutes or until edges are light brown. Cool on cookie sheet for 1 minute and remove to cooling rack.

◆ Cool for several minutes, then press surface into sugar-cinnamon mixture.

CHOCOLATE-DIPPED MALTED MILK COOKIES

The taste of malted milk balls in a cookie?
Unbelievable! These round, crisp cookies have the
color of the inside of a malted milk ball and with the
chocolate coating on one side, taste like them too.

1 (17 OUNCE) SUGAR COOKIE MIX	1 (487 G)
½ CUP MALTED MILK POWDER	125 ML
1 EGG	1
½ CUP (1 STICK) BUTTER, MELTED	125 ML
1 ½ CUPS MILK CHOCOLATE CHIPS	375 ML
1 TABLESPOON SHORTENING	15 ML

◆ Preheat oven to 375° (190° C). In medium bowl, combine cookie mix, malted milk powder, egg and butter. Mix well.

◆ Use your hands to roll heaping teaspoonfuls dough into balls and place 3 inches (7.6 cm) apart on ungreased cookie sheet.

◆ Bake for 9 to 11 minutes, just until edges brown. Cool cookies on baking pan for 1 minute before transferring to cooling rack.

◆ In small saucepan over low heat, melt chocolate in shortening stir constantly. Remove from heat.

◆ Coat cooled cookie by tilting pan and dipping half of cookie into chocolate glaze. Gently shake off excess chocolate and place cookie on wax paper.

◆ Leave cookies on wax paper for about 1 hour to set chocolate. Store cookies in covered container in single layers with wax paper between them.

MY NOTES

Stir Up Some Dreamy Delights... With Bars

Cake, brownie and cookie mixes can be used to create an amazing assortment of delicious bars—everything from cake-like bars to chewy, dense, brownie-like bars, to crunchy-topped, jam-filled bars. The following pages contain recipes covering a range of flavor combinations.

The great thing about using a mix for bar cookies is ease of use. Just like the cakes, most of the recipes that follow use a few additional ingredients to create different desserts in a snap.

CHOCOLATE-PECAN PIE SQUARES

This is a versatile little dessert—the bars are great by themselves, but even better with the Caramel Sauce and Chocolate Whipped Cream. For a really decadent taste treat, serve them warm with a scoop of vanilla ice cream on top and a little warm caramel sauce.

1 (17 OUNCE) SUGAR COOKIE MIX	1 (487 G)
4 EGGS, DIVIDED	4
¾ CUP (1 ½ STICKS) BUTTER, DIVIDED	180 ML
½ TEASPOON CINNAMON	2 ML
1 (1 OUNCE) SQUARE SEMI-SWEET CHOCOLATE	1 (28 G)
1 ½ CUPS PACKED BROWN SUGAR	375 ML
2 TABLESPOONS BOURBON	15 ML
1 TEASPOON VANILLA	5 ML
1 CUP COARSELY CHOPPED PECANS	250 ML

◆ Preheat oven to 350° (176° C). Melt ½ cup (125 mL) butter in small saucepan. In medium bowl, combine cookie mix, 1 egg, melted butter and cinnamon.

◆ Spread batter in bottom of lightly greased, floured 9 x 13-inch (23 x 33 cm) baking pan. Bake for 15 minutes until light brown around edges.

◆ In small saucepan, combine remaining butter and chocolate. Cook over low heat, stirring frequently, until both melt. Immediately remove from heat and cool slightly.

◆ In medium bowl, combine remaining eggs, brown sugar, bourbon and vanilla. Add cooled chocolate mixture and blend well. Stir in pecans.

◆ Pour mixture over cookie crust and bake for 15 to 20 minutes. (Check after 15 minutes; if pecans are brown, remove from oven. Do not over bake.)

(CONTINUED ON NEXT PAGE.)

(CONTINUED)

(You may use prepared caramel sauce or make the recipe below. It's a cinch to make and will only take you about 5 minutes.)

CARAMEL SAUCE:

6 TABLESPOONS BUTTER	**90 ML**
¾ CUP PACKED BROWN SUGAR	**180 ML**
½ CUP WHIPPING CREAM	**125 ML**

◆ Combine butter and brown sugar in medium saucepan. Cook over medium heat, stirring constantly, until sugar dissolves.

◆ Gradually add cream, stirring well after each addition, until mixture comes to a boil.

◆ Boil for 1 to 2 minutes and remove from heat. (Makes a little over 1 cup (250 mL).) Store tightly covered in refrigerator and use as needed.

CHOCOLATE WHIPPED CREAM:

½ CUP WHIPPING CREAM	**125 ML**
1 TABLESPOON POWDERED SUGAR	**15 ML**
1 TABLESPOON COCOA	**15 ML**

◆ In small chilled bowl, combine whipping cream, powdered sugar and cocoa; beat on high speed until stiff peaks form and stop to scrape bowl occasionally as you beat. (Makes ¾ cup (180 mL).)

LEMON-RASPBERRY CRUMB BARS

The raspberries are not only colorful but they also add a nice tart flavor that goes well with the sweet lemon topping.

1 (18 OUNCE) YELLOW OR WHITE CAKE MIX WITH OR WITHOUT PUDDING	**1 (520 G)**
½ CUP (1 STICK) BUTTER, SOFTENED	**125 ML**
1 EGG	**1**
1 (14 OUNCE) CAN SWEETENED CONDENSED MILK	**1 (420 G)**
½ CUP FRESH LEMON JUICE	**125 ML**
½ PINT FRESH RASPBERRIES	**500 ML**

◆ Preheat oven to 350° (176° C). In large bowl, combine cake mix, butter and egg. Blend on low speed until crumbly. (Do not over mix or mixture will become sticky.)

◆ Reserve 2 cups (500 mL) crumb mixture and place remainder in greased 9 x 13-inch (23 x 33 cm) baking pan. Use fingers or turner to press mixture evenly into bottom of pan. Bake for 15 minutes.

◆ While crust is baking, prepare topping. In medium bowl, combine sweetened condensed milk with lemon juice. Stir until well blended. (Mixture will thicken as you stir.)

◆ Arrange raspberries evenly over surface of partially cooked crust.

◆ Pour lemon mixture over raspberries as evenly as possible. (Coverage will be thin in some places.) Sprinkle reserved crumb mixture on top.

◆ Bake for 20 minutes more or until light brown on top. Cool and cut into bars. Keep refrigerated.

CHERRY-ALMOND BARS

*These bars are moist and bursting with cherry flavor.
When I made them for my husband's friends at work,
they raved about them. You can actually make these a
couple of days ahead, because they keep very well.*

1 (18 OUNCE) WHITE CAKE MIX	**1 (520 G)**
⅓ CUP (5 ⅓ TABLESPOONS) BUTTER, SOFTENED	**80 ML**
1 (12 OUNCE) CAN CHERRY PIE FILLING	**1 (340 G)**
1 CUP GROUND ALMONDS	**250 ML**
1 CUP POWDERED SUGAR	**250 ML**
1 TEASPOON ALMOND EXTRACT	**5 ML**
4 EGG WHITES	**4**

◆ Preheat oven to 350° (176° C). In large bowl, combine cake mix and butter. Beat on low speed until blended (mixture will be crumbly); reserve ½ cup (125 mL) for topping. Press remaining mixture into bottom of greased 9 x 13-inch (23 x 33 cm) baking pan.

◆ Spread cherry filling gently over mixture as evenly as possible. (It will be thin in some places.)

◆ In same bowl, combine almonds, powdered sugar, almond extract and egg whites; beat at high speed for 4 minutes. Pour evenly over cherry filling.

◆ Sprinkle ½ cup (125 mL) reserved crumbs over egg white mixture.

◆ Bake for 20 to 25 minutes or until light brown. Cool and cut into bars.

PECAN PIE BARS

These scrumptious bars have a cake-like texture and are loaded with pecan pie flavor. I didn't realize how popular these had become in my family until my father requested them instead of a traditional cake for his birthday!

CRUST:

1 (18 OUNCE) YELLOW CAKE MIX	1 (520 G)
1 EGG	1
¼ CUP (½ STICK) BUTTER, SOFTENED	60 ML
1 CUP SHREDDED COCONUT	250 ML
½ CUP FINELY CHOPPED PECANS	125 ML

FILLING:

1 CUP SUGAR	250 ML
3 EGGS	3
½ TEASPOON SALT	2 ML
1 CUP CORN SYRUP	250 ML
¼ CUP (½ STICK) BUTTER, MELTED	60 ML
1 TEASPOON VANILLA	5 ML
2 CUPS CHOPPED PECANS	500 ML

◆ Preheat oven to 350° (176° C). In large bowl, combine cake mix, egg, butter, coconut and pecans. Beat on low speed until well blended. (Mixture will be crumbly.)

◆ Press mixture into bottom of greased, floured 9 x 13-inch (23 x 33 cm) baking pan. Bake for about 13 minutes (edges should be light brown, but not too dark), and remove from oven.

◆ While crust is baking, prepare filling. In medium bowl, combine sugar, eggs, salt, corn syrup, butter and vanilla. Beat on medium high speed until well blended and fluffy. Stir in pecans.

◆ Pour filling over hot crust and return to oven. Bake for 25 to 30 minutes until edges are brown and center sets. Cool and cut into bars.

ORANGE-WALNUT BARS

1 (17 OUNCE) OATMEAL COOKIE MIX	1 (487 G)
1 TEASPOON CINNAMON	5 ML
⅓ CUP VEGETABLE OIL	80 ML
3 TABLESPOONS WATER	45 ML
5 EGGS, DIVIDED	5
2 CUPS SUGAR	500 ML
2 TABLESPOONS ORANGE ZEST	30 ML
¼ CUP ORANGE JUICE	60 ML
1 TEASPOON BAKING POWDER	5 ML
½ TEASPOON SALT	2 ML
½ CUP CHOPPED WALNUTS	125 ML
1 CUP SHREDDED COCONUT	250 ML

◆ Preheat oven to 350° (176° C). In medium bowl, combine cookie mix, cinnamon, oil, water and 1 egg. Mix well.

◆ With hands (or spatula) press mixture evenly into bottom of greased, floured 9 x 13-inch (23 x 33 cm) baking pan. Bake for 20 minutes. Remove from oven.

◆ In large bowl, combine sugar, orange zest, orange juice, baking powder, salt and remaining eggs.

◆ Beat with mixer on high speed for about 3 minutes until light and fluffy.

◆ Stir in walnuts and coconut. Pour over crust.

◆ Bake for 25 minutes. Remove from oven and cool completely. Cut into bars.

LEMON-APRICOT BARS

Lemon lovers everywhere—beware! Once you get
started on these delicious bars, you won't be able to
stop. They have a crisp crust with a gooey lemon
filling spiked with the tang of apricots.

1 (17 OUNCE) SUGAR COOKIE MIX	1 (487 G)
½ CUP (1 STICK) BUTTER, MELTED	125 ML
⅓ CUP FINELY CHOPPED PECANS	80 ML
5 EGGS, DIVIDED	5
½ CUP SHREDDED COCONUT	125 ML
2 CUPS SUGAR	500 ML
2 TABLESPOONS LEMON ZEST	30 ML
¼ CUP FRESH LEMON JUICE	60 ML
1 TEASPOON BAKING POWDER	5 ML
½ TEASPOON SALT	2 ML
1 CUP SHREDDED COCONUT	250 ML
½ CUP CHOPPED DRIED APRICOTS	125 ML

◆ Preheat oven to 350° (176° C). In medium bowl, combine
cookie mix, butter, pecans and 1 egg. Mix well. Stir in coconut.

◆ With hands (or spatula) press mixture evenly into bottom of
greased, floured 9 x 13-inch (23 x 33 cm) baking pan. Bake for
20 minutes. Remove from oven.

(CONTINUED ON NEXT PAGE.)

(CONTINUED)

◆ In large bowl, combine sugar, lemon zest, lemon juice, baking powder, salt and remaining eggs.

◆ Beat with mixer on high speed for about 3 minutes until light and fluffy. Stir in coconut and apricots. Pour over crust.

◆ Bake for 25 minutes or until no indentation remains when you press the top lightly.

◆ Remove from oven and cool completely. Cut into bars.

These bars are so yummy (and easy to make), I started thinking of other flavor combinations faster than I could make them! The two recipes that follow are variations that are just as good. These are so rich, they will satisfy any sweet tooth.

PINEAPPLE-CHERRY BARS

1 (17 OUNCE) SUGAR COOKIE MIX	1 (487 G)
½ CUP (1 STICK) BUTTER, MELTED	125 ML
5 EGGS, DIVIDED	5
⅓ CUP CHOPPED ALMONDS	80 ML
1 (8 OUNCE) CAN CRUSHED PINEAPPLE,	
WITH JUICE	1 (228 G)
2 CUPS SUGAR	500 ML
½ TEASPOON ALMOND EXTRACT	2 ML
1 TEASPOON BAKING POWDER	5 ML
½ TEASPOON SALT	2 ML
1 CUP COCONUT	250 ML
½ CUP MARASCHINO CHERRIES,	
WELL DRAINED, QUARTERED	125 ML

◆ Preheat oven to 350° (176° C). In medium bowl, combine cookie mix, butter, 1 egg and almonds. Mix well.

◆ With hands (or spatula) press mixture evenly into bottom of greased, floured 9 x 13-inch (23 x 33 cm) baking pan. Bake for 20 minutes. Remove from oven.

◆ Drain pineapple juice and save ¼ cup (60 mL) juice. In large bowl, combine sugar, pineapple juice, almond extract, baking powder, salt and remaining eggs.

◆ Beat with mixer on high speed for about 3 minutes until light and fluffy. Stir in pineapple, coconut and cherries. Pour over crust.

◆ Bake for 25 minutes. Remove from oven and cool completely. Cut into bars.

CHERRY-CHOCOLATE BARS

1 (18 OUNCE) DEVIL'S FOOD CAKE MIX	**1 (520 G)**
1 (20 OUNCE) CAN CHERRY PIE FILLING	**1 (570 G)**
2 EGGS	**2**
1 CUP SEMI-SWEET OR MILK CHOCOLATE CHIPS	**250 ML**

◆ Preheat oven to 350° (176° C). In large bowl, combine all ingredients and blend well.

◆ Pour batter into greased and floured 9 x 13-inch (23 x 33 cm) baking pan.

◆ Bake for 25 to 30 minutes or until cake tester comes out clean. Cool and frost with *Chocolate Cream Cheese Frosting*.

CHOCOLATE CREAM CHEESE FROSTING:

3 (1 OUNCE) SQUARES SEMI-SWEET CHOCOLATE,	
MELTED	**3 (28 G)**
1 (3 OUNCE) PACKAGE CREAM CHEESE,	
SOFTENED	**1 (85 G)**
½ TEASPOON VANILLA	**2 ML**
1 ¼ CUPS POWDERED SUGAR	**310 ML**

◆ In medium bowl, beat chocolate with cream cheese and vanilla.

◆ Gradually beat in powdered sugar until frosting is smooth and well blended.

HONEY-NUT OATMEAL-JAM BARS

½ CUP BUTTER, SOFTENED	125 ML
½ CUP PACKED BROWN SUGAR	125 ML
1¾ CUPS FLOUR	430 ML
PINCH SALT	
½ TEASPOON BAKING SODA	2 ML
4 (2 OUNCE) HONEY-NUT	
INSTANT OATMEAL PACKETS	4 (57 G)
¾ CUP STRAWBERRY JAM	180 ML

◆ Preheat oven to 400° (204° C). In large bowl, cream butter and brown sugar.

◆ Add flour, salt, baking soda and oatmeal; mix well. (Mixture will be crumbly.)

◆ Press half of mixture firmly into bottom of greased 8 x 8-inch (20 x 20 cm) baking pan. Spread jam over mixture.

◆ Top with remaining crumbled mixture. Bake for 25 to 30 minutes or until light brown. Cool slightly and cut into bars.

PUMPKIN BARS

*With their spicy flavor, these bars are a perfect
snack for the Thanksgiving holidays.*

½ CUP (1 STICK) BUTTER, MELTED	**125 ML**
1 CUP PACKED LIGHT BROWN SUGAR	**250 ML**
1 CUP CANNED PUMPKIN	**250 ML**
1 ½ CUPS FLOUR	**375 ML**
½ TEASPOON BAKING SODA	**2 ML**
2 (2 OUNCE) CINNAMON SPICE	
INSTANT OATMEAL PACKETS	**2 (57 G)**
½ CUP CHOPPED PECANS	**125 ML**

◆ Preheat oven to 350° (176° C). In medium bowl, combine butter, sugar and pumpkin; mix well.

◆ In separate bowl, combine flour, baking soda, oatmeal and pecans; stir to blend. Add to pumpkin mixture and mix thoroughly.

◆ Spread evenly in greased 9 x 13-inch (23 x 33 cm) baking pan, and bake for 16 to 18 minutes. Immediately upon removing from oven, pour glaze over bars. Cool and cut.

GLAZE:

1 CUP POWDERED SUGAR	**250 ML**
3 TABLESPOONS ORANGE JUICE	**45 ML**

◆ In small bowl, blend powdered sugar and orange juice.

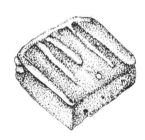

LEMON-GLAZED PECAN BARS

*The pecan and lemon combination in these bars is a
little unusual, but really very good. These bars are
very similar to pecan pie with a sweet cookie crust.
Because they hold together well, they're very portable
and make a good dessert to take to a get-together.*

1 (17 OUNCE) PACKAGE SUGAR COOKIE MIX	1 (487 G)
3 EGGS	3
1 CUP PACKED DARK BROWN SUGAR	250 ML
1 CUP CHOPPED PECANS, TOASTED	250 ML
1 CUP SHREDDED COCONUT	250 ML
2 TEASPOONS VANILLA	10 ML
½ CUP POWDERED SUGAR	125 ML
¼ CUP FRESH LEMON JUICE	60 ML
ZEST OF 1 SMALL LEMON	1

◆ Preheat oven to 350° (176° C). Prepare cookie dough according to package directions. Press cookie dough evenly in bottom of lightly greased, floured 9 x 13-inch (23 x 33 cm) baking pan.

◆ Bake for 15 minutes or until light brown around edges. Remove from oven and cool for about 10 minutes.

◆ While crust is baking, in medium bowl combine eggs, brown sugar, pecans, coconut and vanilla. Mix well.

◆ Pour over warm crust and bake for another 15 to 20 minutes or until slightly brown on top.

◆ To make glaze, in small bowl combine powdered sugar, lemon juice and lemon zest. Mix well. Either brush or drizzle glaze over bars while they are still warm from the oven. Cool and cut into bars.

For toasting pecans, see page 91.

180

BROWNIE-BOTTOM CHEESECAKE WITH CHOCOLATE FROSTING

1 (18 OUNCE) DEVIL'S FOOD CAKE MIX WITH OR WITHOUT PUDDING	1 (520 G)
½ CUP BUTTER	125 ML
3 EGGS, DIVIDED	3
2 (8 OUNCE) PACKAGES CREAM CHEESE, SOFTENED	2 (228 G)
¾ CUP SUGAR	180 ML

◆ Preheat oven to 325° (163° C). In large bowl, combine cake mix, butter and 1 egg; blend well. Press mixture into bottom of greased 9 x 13-inch (23 x 33 cm) baking pan.

◆ In medium bowl, combine remaining eggs, cream cheese and sugar. Beat until mixture is smooth and well blended.

◆ Pour mixture over cake mix and bake for 40 to 45 minutes until edges are very light brown. Cool and ice with Chocolate Frosting.

CHOCOLATE FROSTING:

1 CUP SEMI-SWEET CHOCOLATE CHIPS	250 ML
1 (8 OUNCE) CONTAINER SOUR CREAM	1 (228 G)

◆ In small saucepan, combine chocolate chips and sour cream.

◆ Cook over low to medium heat, stirring constantly, until chocolate melts and mixture is smooth. Remove from heat and cool until just warm to the touch.

CHOCOLATE-TOPPED TOFFEE BARS

1 (18 OUNCE) WHITE CAKE MIX	1 (520 G)
¼ CUP (½ STICK) BUTTER, MELTED	60 ML
¼ CUP PACKED BROWN SUGAR	60 ML
¼ CUP MILK	60 ML
2 EGGS	2
1 ½ CUPS TOFFEE CHIPS	375 ML
¾ CUP CHOPPED PECANS	180 ML

◆ Preheat oven to 375° (190° C). In large bowl, combine cake mix, butter, brown sugar, milk and eggs.

◆ Beat on low speed to blend, about 2 minutes. Stir in toffee chips and stir in pecans.

◆ Spread batter in greased, floured 9 x 13-inch (23 x 33 cm) baking dish. Bake for 20 to 25 minutes, or until light brown.

◆ When cool, drizzle with *Chocolate Glaze* on next page.

(CONTINUED ON NEXT PAGE.)

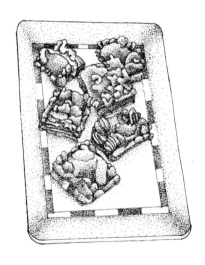

(CONTINUED)

CHOCOLATE GLAZE:

½ CUP MILK CHOCOLATE CHIPS	125 ML
2 TEASPOONS BUTTER OR SHORTENING	10 ML

◆ Melt chocolate and shortening together in small saucepan or in microwave at half power (stirring every 30 seconds until chocolate melts and mixture is smooth).

VARIATION:

For a really chewy, moist bar, try adding the following topping before baking. You'll need to add an additional 5 minutes to the baking time, but they turn out so rich!

3 TABLESPOONS BUTTER, MELTED	45 ML
1 CUP PACKED BROWN SUGAR	250 ML
1 CUP SHREDDED COCONUT	250 ML

◆ Combine butter with brown sugar and mix well. Stir in coconut until it is thoroughly coated.

◆ Sprinkle over batter just before baking. When cool, drizzle with chocolate glaze.

BUTTERSCOTCH BARS

1 (18 OUNCE) WHITE CAKE MIX	1 (520 G)
1 (3 OUNCE) INSTANT BUTTERSCOTCH	
PUDDING MIX	1 (85 G)
1 CUP MILK	250 ML
1 EGG	1
1 CUP CHOPPED PECANS	250 ML
¾ CUP BUTTERSCOTCH BAKING CHIPS	180 ML

◆ Preheat oven to 350° (176° C). In large bowl, combine cake mix, pudding mix, milk and egg.

◆ Beat on low speed until well blended (about 1 minute).

◆ Stir in pecans and spread batter in greased, floured 9 x 13-inch (23 x 33 cm) baking pan.

◆ Sprinkle butterscotch chips evenly over surface, and press lightly into batter.

◆ Bake for 30 to 35 minutes until cake tester comes out clean.

(CONTINUED)

CHOCOLATE GLAZE:

½ CUP MILK CHOCOLATE CHIPS	125 ML
2 TEASPOONS BUTTER OR SHORTENING	10 ML

◆ Melt chocolate and shortening together in small saucepan or in microwave at half power (stirring every 30 seconds until chocolate melts and mixture is smooth).

VARIATION:

For a really chewy, moist bar, try adding the following topping before baking. You'll need to add an additional 5 minutes to the baking time, but they turn out so rich!

3 TABLESPOONS BUTTER, MELTED	45 ML
1 CUP PACKED BROWN SUGAR	250 ML
1 CUP SHREDDED COCONUT	250 ML

◆ Combine butter with brown sugar and mix well. Stir in coconut until it is thoroughly coated.

◆ Sprinkle over batter just before baking. When cool, drizzle with chocolate glaze.

BUTTERSCOTCH BARS

1 (18 OUNCE) WHITE CAKE MIX	**1 (520 G)**
1 (3 OUNCE) INSTANT BUTTERSCOTCH	
PUDDING MIX	**1 (85 G)**
1 CUP MILK	**250 ML**
1 EGG	**1**
1 CUP CHOPPED PECANS	**250 ML**
¾ CUP BUTTERSCOTCH BAKING CHIPS	**180 ML**

◆ Preheat oven to 350° (176° C). In large bowl, combine cake mix, pudding mix, milk and egg.

◆ Beat on low speed until well blended (about 1 minute).

◆ Stir in pecans and spread batter in greased, floured 9 x 13-inch (23 x 33 cm) baking pan.

◆ Sprinkle butterscotch chips evenly over surface, and press lightly into batter.

◆ Bake for 30 to 35 minutes until cake tester comes out clean.

CHOCOLATE-DREAM BARS

1 (18 OUNCE) GERMAN CHOCOLATE CAKE MIX	1 (520 G)
3 CUPS QUICK-COOKING OATS	750 ML
1 CUP (2 STICKS) BUTTER, MELTED	250 ML
1 (14 OUNCE) CAN SWEETENED	
CONDENSED MILK	1 (420 G)
1 CUP SEMI-SWEET CHOCOLATE CHIPS	250 L
1 CUP SHREDDED COCONUT	250 ML
¾ CUP CHOPPED PECANS	180 ML

◆ Preheat oven to 375° (190° C). In large bowl, combine cake mix and oats. Mix well.

◆ Add butter and beat mixture on low speed until it clumps together and all dry mix is moist.

◆ Press half of this mixture in greased 9 x 13-inch (23 x 33 cm) baking pan. Pour condensed milk evenly over batter.

◆ Sprinkle chocolate chips, coconut and pecans evenly over milk.

◆ Crumble remaining mixture over and bake for 20 minutes. Cool well before cutting into bars.

LEMON-BUTTERMILK BARS

These bars are one of my all-time favorites for their delicious flavor! Their delicate lemon taste, very moist texture and crispy crust makes them taste a lot like buttermilk pie.

1 (18 OUNCE) LEMON CAKE MIX (WITH PUDDING), DIVIDED	1 (520 G)
4 EGGS, DIVIDED	4
2 TABLESPOONS VEGETABLE OIL	30 ML
1 CUP BUTTERMILK	250 ML
½ CUP BUTTER, MELTED	125 ML
¾ CUP SUGAR	180 ML
1 TEASPOON VANILLA	5 ML

◆ Preheat oven to 350° (176° C). Reserve 1 cup (250 mL) dry cake mix and set aside.

◆ In large bowl, combine remaining cake mix, 1 egg and oil and blend well. Press batter into bottom of greased 9 x 13-inch (23 x 33 cm) baking pan.

◆ In medium bowl, beat remaining eggs, buttermilk, butter, sugar and vanilla until well blended.

◆ Slowly add reserved cake mix and beat on medium speed until mixture is smooth, about 2 minutes.

◆ Pour over batter in cake pan, and bake for 35 to 40 minutes until light brown on top. Cool and cut into bars.

NO-BAKE CHOCOLATE-OATMEAL BARS

These easy to make bars are hard to resist and disappear as fast as you make them.

2 CUPS SUGAR	**500 ML**
½ CUP SWEETENED CONDENSED MILK	**125 ML**
1 (1 OUNCE) SQUARE UNSWEETENED	
BAKING CHOCOLATE	**1 (28 G)**
½ CUP (1 STICK) BUTTER	**125 ML**
1 TEASPOON VANILLA	**5 ML**
½ CUP CREAMY PEANUT BUTTER	**125 ML**
PINCH OF SALT	
½ CUP CHOPPED PECANS	**125 ML**
5 (2 OUNCE) PACKETS MAPLE BROWN SUGAR	
INSTANT OATMEAL	**5 (57 G)**

◆ In heavy saucepan, bring sugar, milk, chocolate and butter to a boil, then immediately remove from heat.

◆ Add vanilla, peanut butter, salt, pecans and oatmeal. Stir well and quickly press into greased 9 x 13-inch (23 x 33 cm) baking dish.

◆ Cool slightly and cut into bars.

CHERRY-CHEESE SQUARES

1 (18 OUNCE) WHITE CAKE MIX WITH PUDDING	1 (520 G)
½ CUP (1 STICK) BUTTER, MELTED	125 ML
½ CUP CHOPPED ALMONDS	125 ML
1 (16 OUNCE) JAR CHERRY PRESERVES, DIVIDED	1 (454 G)
1 (8 OUNCE) PACKAGE CREAM CHEESE, SOFTENED	1 (228 G)
¼ CUP SUGAR	60 ML
2 TABLESPOONS FLOUR	30 ML
1 EGG	1
1 TEASPOON ALMOND EXTRACT	5 ML
½ CUP SHREDDED COCONUT	125 ML

◆ Preheat oven to 350° (176° C). In large bowl, combine cake mix and butter. Beat on low speed until mixture is crumbly. Stir in almonds. Reserve 1 cup (250 mL) mixture.

◆ Press remaining mixture into bottom of greased 9 x 13-inch baking pan. Spread 1 cup (250 mL) cherry preserves over mixture to within ½ inch of edges of pan.

◆ In medium bowl, beat cream cheese until smooth and add remaining preserves, sugar, flour, egg and almond extract.

◆ Continue to beat, scraping bowl as necessary, until mixture is smooth. Gently spread on top of preserves to edge of pan.

◆ Combine coconut with reserved crumb mixture and sprinkle over cream cheese.

◆ Bake for 25 to 30 minutes or until light brown on top. Cool completely and cut into squares.

VARIATION:
If you like the taste of citrus, you may make this same recipe with apricot preserves and a lemon cake mix. Just substitute apricot preserves for the cherry preserves and a lemon cake mix for the white. You may also use clear vanilla flavoring instead of the almond if you want.

190

APRICOT-OATMEAL BARS

These bars are an example of how just a few ingredients (4 to be exact) added to a cake mix can produce a tasty treat.

1 (18 OUNCE) YELLOW CAKE MIX	1 (520 G)
3 CUPS OLD-FASHION OATS	750 ML
¾ CUP CHOPPED PECANS	180 ML
1 CUP (2 STICKS) BUTTER, MELTED	250 ML
1 ½ CUPS APRICOT JAM	375 ML

◆ Preheat oven to 375° (190° C). In large bowl, combine cake mix, oats, pecans and butter. Mix well until entire mixture is crumbly.

◆ Press half of mixture evenly into bottom of greased 9 x 13-inch (23 x 33 cm) baking pan.

◆ Spread apricot jam evenly over surface and sprinkle remaining half of mixture evenly over jam.

◆ Bake for 20 minutes or until well browned on top.

LEMON-CHEESECAKE BARS WITH WHITE CHOCOLATE FROSTING

1 (18 OUNCE) LEMON CAKE MIX WITH PUDDING	1 (520 G)
½ CUP (1 STICK) BUTTER, SOFTENED	125 ML
3 EGGS, DIVIDED	3
2 (8 OUNCE) PACKAGES CREAM CHEESE, SOFTENED	2 (228 G)
1 TEASPOON VANILLA	5 ML
1 TEASPOON LEMON EXTRACT	5 ML
2 CUPS POWDERED SUGAR	500 ML

◆ Preheat oven to 325° (163° C). In large bowl, combine cake mix, butter and 1 egg. Beat on low speed until well blended. Spread batter into bottom of greased 9 x 13-inch (23 x 33 cm) baking pan.

◆ In medium bowl, combine 2 eggs, cream cheese, vanilla, lemon extract and sugar.

◆ Beat on low speed to blend and beat on medium speed until mixture is smooth (from 1 to 2 minutes).

◆ Pour over cake batter; bake for 40 to 45 minutes. Cool and frost with *White Chocolate Frosting*.

WHITE CHOCOLATE FROSTING:

1 CUP WHITE CHOCOLATE BAKING CHIPS	250 ML
1 (8 OUNCE) CONTAINER SOUR CREAM	1 (228 G)

◆ In small saucepan, heat white chocolate and sour cream over low to medium heat, stirring constantly, until chocolate melts and mixture is smooth.

◆ Remove from heat and cool to lukewarm. Frost cake.

MARBLED-CHEESECAKE BARS

1 (18 OUNCE) YELLOW CAKE MIX WITH PUDDING, DIVIDED	1 (520 G)
4 EGGS, DIVIDED	4
2 TABLESPOONS VEGETABLE OIL	30 ML
1 (8 OUNCE) PACKAGE CREAM CHEESE, SOFTENED	1 (228 G)
½ CUP SUGAR	125 ML
1 ½ CUPS MILK	375 ML
1 TEASPOON VANILLA	5 ML
2 (1 OUNCE) SQUARES SWEET BAKING CHOCOLATE, MELTED	2 (28 G)

◆ Preheat oven to 325° (163° C).. Reserve 1 cup (250 mL) dry cake mix. Set aside. Combine remaining cake mix, 1 egg and oil. Mix well (mixture will be crumbly).

◆ Using spatula press mixture firmly into bottom of greased 9 x 13-inch (23 x 33 cm) baking pan.

◆ In large bowl, beat cream cheese and sugar until light and fluffy. Add 3 eggs and reserved cake mix; blend well.

◆ Slowly add milk and vanilla and beat on medium speed until smooth and thoroughly blended (about 2 minutes).

◆ Remove 1 cup (250 mL) cream cheese mixture and pour remainder over batter in baking pan.

◆ Add chocolate to reserved cream cheese mixture and blend well. Pour in zig-zag fashion over cream cheese mixture in baking pan and use butter knife to swirl, creating a marbled effect.

◆ Bake for 50 to 55 minutes until knife inserted into center comes out clean. Cool and refrigerate until serving.

CHERRY-CHEESECAKE BARS

*The sugar cookie mix makes a delicious, sweet crust for
this cheesecake, which is big enough for a hungry crowd.*

1 (17 OUNCE) PACKAGE SUGAR COOKIE MIX	1 (487 G)
1 (8 OUNCE) PACKAGE CREAM CHEESE, SOFTENED	1 (228 G)
1 ½ CUPS MILK	375 ML
2 TABLESPOONS SUGAR	30 ML
½ TEASPOON CLEAR VANILLA	2 ML
1 (3 OUNCE) LEMON INSTANT PUDDING MIX	1 (85 G)
1 (20 OUNCE) CAN CHERRY PIE FILLING	1 (570 G)

◆ Preheat oven to 375° (190° C). Prepare cookie dough
according to package directions.

◆ Press cookie dough evenly into bottom of greased 9 x 13-inch
(23 x 33 cm) baking pan.

◆ Bake for 15 minutes until center is set and edges brown. Remove
from oven and cool.

◆ In medium bowl, beat cream cheese, milk, sugar and vanilla until
mixture is smooth.

◆ Add pudding mix and beat on low speed about 1 minute until
mixture thickens.

◆ Spread mixture over cooled crust and refrigerate for at least
2 hours. Just before serving, spoon cherry
pie filling over top. Keep refrigerated.

MAPLE-PECAN CHEESECAKE BARS

CRUST:
1 (17 OUNCE) SUGAR COOKIE MIX	1 (487 G)
¾ CUP CHOPPED PECANS	180 ML
1 EGG	1
½ CUP (1 STICK) BUTTER, SOFTENED	125 ML

TOPPING:
2 (8 OUNCE) PACKAGES CREAM CHEESE, SOFTENED	2 (228 G)
1 CUP PACKED BROWN SUGAR	250 ML
2 TABLESPOONS FLOUR	30 ML
2 EGGS	2
2 TEASPOONS MAPLE EXTRACT	10 ML
¾ CUP PECAN HALVES	180 ML
2 (1 OUNCE) SQUARES SWEETENED CHOCOLATE, MELTED	2 (28 G)

◆ Preheat oven to 350° (176° C). In medium bowl, blend cookie mix, pecans, egg and butter until well blended.

◆ Press into bottom of greased 9 x 13-inch (23 x 33 cm) baking dish. Bake for 20 minutes. Remove from oven.

◆ Reduce oven temperature to 325° (163° C). In large bowl, beat cream cheese and sugar until light and fluffy.

◆ Gradually add flour, eggs and maple extract, mixing only blended.

◆ Pour mixture over warm crust and arrange pecan halves attractively on surface. Place back in oven and bake for 15 minutes.

◆ Remove from oven and cool. Drizzle melted chocolate over top. Cut into bars. Keep refrigerated.

PEANUT BUTTER BARS

1 (18 OUNCE) GERMAN CHOCOLATE CAKE MIX	1 (520 G)
½ CUP PACKED BROWN SUGAR	125 ML
1 EGG	1
¼ CUP MILK	60 ML
2 TABLESPOONS BUTTER	30 ML
½ CUP PEANUT BUTTER	125 ML

◆ Preheat oven to 325° (163° C). In large bowl, combine cake mix, sugar, egg and milk.

◆ Melt butter with peanut butter and mix well. Add to cake mix ingredients in large bowl. Beat on low speed just enough to blend mixture.

◆ Press into bottom of greased, floured 9 x 13-inch (23 x 33 cm) baking pan. Bake for 25 to 30 minutes or until cake tester comes out clean. Cool and frost with *Peanut Butter Frosting*.

PEANUT BUTTER FROSTING:

2 TABLESPOONS BUTTER	30 ML
2 TABLESPOONS CREAMY PEANUT BUTTER	30 ML
3 TABLESPOONS LIGHT CORN SYRUP	45 ML
1 TEASPOON VANILLA	5 ML
1 CUP SEMI-SWEET CHOCOLATE CHIPS	250 ML
¼ CUP POWDERED SUGAR	60 ML

◆ Heat butter, peanut butter, corn syrup and vanilla in small saucepan over low heat, stirring frequently until mixture is smooth.

◆ Remove from heat, stir in chocolate chips and beat until chocolate melts and mixture is smooth. Add powdered sugar and blend well.

STRAWBERRY-CREAM CHEESE BARS

*If you like cheesecake or pastries with cheese filling,
you'll really like these bars. With the consistency
of a brownie when baked, these bars come out
of the oven topped with a thin layer of cheese
similar to what you'd find in a cheese danish.*

1 (18 OUNCE) STRAWBERRY CAKE MIX	
(WITH OR WITHOUT PUDDING)	1 (520 G)
½ CUP (1 STICK) BUTTER	125 ML
3 EGGS, DIVIDED	3
1 (8 OUNCE) PACKAGE CREAM CHEESE, SOFTENED	1 (228 G)
2 CUPS POWDERED SUGAR	500 ML

◆ Preheat oven to 325° (163° C). In large bowl, combine cake mix, butter and 1 egg and blend well.

◆ Press mixture into bottom of greased 9 x 13-inch (23 x 33 cm) baking pan.

◆ In medium bowl, beat cream cheese, 2 eggs and sugar until mixture is smooth and well blended.

◆ Pour mixture over cake mix batter, and bake for 30 to 35 minutes until light brown on top.

PINEAPPLE-MACADAMIA NUT BARS

These cake-like bars are chock-full of macadamia-nut flavor.

1 (18 OUNCE) WHITE CAKE MIX	**1 (520 G)**
¼ CUP (½ STICK) BUTTER, MELTED	**60 ML**
¼ CUP PACKED BROWN SUGAR	**60 ML**
1 (8 OUNCE) CAN CRUSHED PINEAPPLE	
WITH JUICE	**1 (228 G)**
2 EGGS	**2**
¾ CUP CHOPPED MACADAMIA NUTS, TOASTED	**180 ML**

◆ Preheat oven to 375° (190° C). Drain pineapple and save ¼ cup (60 mL) plus 2 tablespoons (30 mL).

◆ In large bowl, combine cake mix, butter, brown sugar, pineapple, ¼ cup (60 mL) pineapple juice and eggs. Beat on low speed or by hand until well blended (about 1 minute).

◆ Stir in macadamia nuts and spread batter into greased, floured 9 x 13-inch (23 x 33 cm) baking pan.

◆ Bake for 20 minutes or until golden brown. Remove from oven, cool slightly and frost with *Pineapple Icing*.

PINEAPPLE ICING:

2 TABLESPOONS BUTTER, SOFTENED	**30 ML**
2 TABLESPOONS RESERVED PINEAPPLE JUICE	**30 ML**
PINCH OF SALT	
2 CUPS POWDERED SUGAR, DIVIDED	**500 ML**

◆ In small bowl, cream butter with pineapple juice, salt and ½ cup (125 mL) powdered sugar.

◆ Add remaining powdered sugar a little at a time, blending well after each addition. Spread on warm bars.

GOOEY SNICKERS BROWNIES

"Gooey" really describes these very dense, rich brownies.

1 (18 OUNCE) GERMAN CHOCOLATE CAKE MIX	**1 (520 G)**
¾ CUP BUTTER, MELTED	**180 ML**
½ CUP EVAPORATED MILK	**125 ML**
4 (2 OUNCE) SNICKERS CANDY BARS	**4 (57 G)**

◆ Preheat oven to 350° (176° C). In large bowl, combine cake mix, butter and evaporated milk. Beat on low speed until they blend (1 to 2 minutes).

◆ Spread half of batter into bottom of greased 9 x 13-inch (23 x 33 cm) baking pan. Bake for 10 minutes.

◆ Remove brownies from oven. Slice Snickers into ⅛-inch pieces and place slices evenly over surface.

◆ Drop remaining half of batter by spoonful over candy bars as evenly as possible.

◆ Place back in oven and bake for 20 minutes. (Brownies will jiggle slightly on top when you remove them from oven.) Cool and cut into bars.

COFFEE AND CREAM BROWNIES

1 (3 OUNCE) PACKAGE CREAM CHEESE, SOFTENED	1 (85 G)
2 TABLESPOONS BUTTER, SOFTENED	30 ML
¼ CUP SUGAR	60 ML
4 EGGS, DIVIDED	4
½ TEASPOON VANILLA	2 ML
1 TABLESPOON FLOUR	15 ML
2 TABLESPOONS INSTANT COFFEE GRANULES	30 ML
¼ CUP WARM WATER	60 ML
1 (20 OUNCE) BOX FAMILY-SIZE BROWNIE MIX	1 (570 G)
½ CUP VEGETABLE OIL	125 ML

◆ Preheat oven to 350° (176° C). Combine cream cheese and butter; blend thoroughly. Add sugar and blend until light and fluffy.

◆ Beat in 1 egg and vanilla, stir in flour and mix well. Set aside.

◆ In medium bowl, dissolve coffee in water. Add brownie mix, remaining eggs and vegetable oil and blend well. Pour half batter into greased 9 x 13-inch (23 x 33 cm) baking dish.

◆ Drop cheese mixture by heaping tablespoons over brownie batter.

◆ Pour remaining batter over cheese mixture and gently swirl butter knife to create marbled effect. Bake for 25 to 30 minutes.

MOUSSE-TOPPED BROWNIES

1 (16 OUNCE) PACKAGE BROWNIE MIX	**1 (454 G)**
¾ CUP HEAVY WHIPPING CREAM	**180 ML**
1 CUP MILK CHOCOLATE CHIPS	**250 ML**
3 EGGS	**3**
⅓ CUP BUTTER	**80 ML**

◆ Preheat oven to 325° (163° C). Prepare brownie batter according to package directions. Put batter in greased 8 x 8-inch (20 x 20 cm) pan.

◆ In small saucepan, heat whipping cream over medium heat until hot, but not boiling.

◆ Stir in chocolate chips and remove from heat. Stir until chocolate completely melts. Set aside.

◆ In medium bowl, combine eggs and butter. Beat at medium speed for several minutes until eggs are frothy.

◆ While beating, gradually add chocolate mixture until well blended.

◆ Pour chocolate mixture over brownie batter and bake for 45 to 50 minutes. Cool completely and cut into bars.

ROCKY ROAD BROWNIES

1 (20 OUNCE) PACKAGE BROWNIE MIX	1 (570 G)
1 CUP MINIATURE MARSHMALLOWS	250 G
1 (11.5 OUNCE) PACKAGE MILK CHOCOLATE OR	
SEMI-SWEET CHOCOLATE CHIPS	1 (328 G)
1 (14 OUNCE) CAN SWEETENED CONDENSED MILK	1 (420 G)
1 CUP COARSELY CHOPPED PECANS	250 ML

◆ Preheat oven to 350° (176° C). Prepare brownies according to package directions for fudge-like brownies, but use 2 eggs instead of 3. Bake for 30 minutes.

◆ Remove from oven and immediately sprinkle marshmallows evenly over surface and cool.

◆ In small saucepan, melt chocolate chips over low heat. Remove from heat and stir in condensed milk. Blend well.

◆ Stir in pecans. Pour evenly over marshmallows. Cool for several hours. Cut into bars.

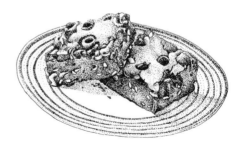

BLACK FOREST CHERRY CAKE BROWNIES

It's hard to beat the flavor of chocolate and cherries. By cutting the cherries in half instead of chopping them, you can really taste the flavor when you bite into them.

1 (20 OUNCE) BOX BROWNIE MIX	**1 (570 G)**
¼ CUP MARASCHINO CHERRY JUICE	**60 ML**
½ CUP VEGETABLE OIL	**125 ML**
3 EGGS	**3**
1 CUP MARASCHINO CHERRIES, HALVED	**250 G**
¾ CUP SEMI-SWEET CHOCOLATE CHIPS	**180 G**

◆ Preheat oven to 350° (176° C). In medium bowl, combine brownie mix, maraschino cherry juice, oil and eggs until well blended. Gently stir in cherry halves and chocolate chips and mix well.

◆ Pour batter into greased, floured 9 x 13-inch (23 x 33 cm) baking dish. Bake for 28 to 30 minutes. Cool and frost with *Cherry Icing.*

CHERRY ICING:

6 TABLESPOONS BUTTER, SOFTENED	**90 ML**
3 CUPS POWDERED SUGAR, DIVIDED	**750 ML**
⅛ TEASPOON ALMOND EXTRACT	**.5 ML**
¼ CUP MARASCHINO CHERRY JUICE	**60 ML**

◆ In medium bowl, cream butter and 1 cup (250 mL) powdered sugar until well mixed.

◆ Add almond extract, cherry juice and remaining sugar alternately, blending well after each addition, until icing is smooth and reaches frosting consistency. Spread icing over cake.

203

MILKY WAY BROWNIES

1 (16 OUNCE) BOX BROWNIE MIX	**1 (454 G)**
3 (2 OUNCE) MILKY WAY CANDY BARS, DIVIDED	**3 (57 G)**
5 TABLESPOONS BUTTER	**75 ML**
1 TEASPOON VANILLA	**5 ML**
¾ CUP POWDERED SUGAR	**180 ML**

◆ Preheat oven to 350° (176° C). Mix brownies according to package directions. Pour half of batter into greased 8 x 8-inch (20 x 20 cm) baking pan.

◆ Slice 1 Milky Way bar into pieces ⅛ inch thick. (Refrigerate candy bar beforehand to make it easier to slice.)

◆ Distribute candy bar slices evenly on batter. Cover with remaining batter and smooth over. Bake for 40 to 42 minutes.

◆ During last 10 minutes of baking time, prepare frosting. Chop remaining 2 candy bars into 1-inch size (2.5 cm) chunks and place in small saucepan.

◆ Add butter and melt over low to medium heat, stirring constantly, until candy bars completely melt and mixture is smooth.

◆ Lower heat to warm and stir in vanilla. Add powdered sugar a little at a time, stirring well with each addition.

◆ Frost brownies soon after removing from oven while still hot.

RASPBERRY-ALMOND CHEESECAKE BROWNIES

1 (20 OUNCE) PACKAGE BROWNIE MIX	**1 (570 G)**
1 (12 OUNCE) CAN RASPBERRY FILLING, DIVIDED	**1 (340 G)**
1 (8 OUNCE) PACKAGE CREAM CHEESE, SOFTENED	**1 (228 G)**
2 TABLESPOONS BUTTER, SOFTENED	**30 ML**
1 TABLESPOON CORNSTARCH	**15 ML**
1 (14 OUNCE) CAN SWEETENED CONDENSED MILK	**1 (420 G)**
1 EGG	**1**
2 TEASPOONS ALMOND EXTRACT	**10 ML**

◆ Preheat oven to 350° (176° C). Prepare batter according to package directions. Add 1 cup (250 mL) raspberry filling to the batter and beat on low speed until mixed.

◆ Pour batter into greased, floured 9 x 13-inch (23 x 33 cm) baking pan.

◆ In medium bowl, beat cream cheese, butter and cornstarch until light and fluffy. While continuing to beat, slowly add condensed milk, egg and almond extract. Beat until well blended and smooth.

◆ Pour cheese mixture over batter. Drop remaining raspberry filling by spoonfuls evenly over cheese mixture.

◆ Be care not to over mix; swirl butter knife or back of spoon gently through mixture to create a marbled effect.

◆ Bake for 40 to 45 minutes or until light brown on top. Cool and keep refrigerated.

CRISPY-TOPPED BROWNIES

These brownies are so good! The brown sugar and
coconut makes a crispy, tasty topping.

1 (20 OUNCE) PACKAGE BROWNIE MIX	**1 (570 G)**
¾ CUP MINI-CHOCOLATE CHIPS	**180 ML**
3 TABLESPOONS BUTTER, MELTED	**45 ML**
1 CUP PACKED BROWN SUGAR	**250 ML**
½ CUP CHOPPED NUTS	**125 ML**
1 CUP SHREDDED COCONUT	**250 ML**

◆ Preheat oven to 350° (176° C). Prepare brownie batter
according to package directions.

◆ Spread prepared batter in greased, floured 9 x 13-inch
(23 x 33 cm) baking pan. Sprinkle chocolate chips evenly over
surface.

◆ In small bowl, combine butter, brown sugar, nuts and coconut;
mix well. Sprinkle mixture over chocolate chips.

◆ Bake for 25 to 30 minutes.

CAPPUCCINO BROWNIES
WITH MOCHA ICING

3 TABLESPOONS INSTANT COFFEE GRANULES	**45 ML**
¼ CUP WARM WATER	**60 ML**
1 (20 OUNCE) PACKAGE BROWNIE MIX	**1 (570 G)**
1 TABLESPOON CINNAMON	**15 ML**
3 EGGS	**3**
½ CUP VEGETABLE OIL	**125 ML**

◆ Preheat oven to 350° (176° C). Stir coffee into water until it dissolves. In medium bowl, combine brownie mix, coffee mixture, cinnamon, eggs and oil.

◆ Beat on low speed until blended. Pour batter into greased, floured 9 x 13-inch (23 x 33 cm) baking pan. Bake for 25 to 30 minutes. Cool and frost with *Mocha Icing*.

MOCHA ICING:

1 TEASPOON INSTANT COFFEE GRANULES	**5 ML**
¼ CUP MILK	**60 ML**
4 OUNCES CREAM CHEESE, SOFTENED	**115 G**
1 (1 POUND) PACKAGE POWDERED SUGAR	**1 (454 G)**

◆ Add coffee to milk and stir until it dissolves.

◆ In small bowl, beat cream cheese and coffee mixture until smooth and creamy.

◆ Slowly add powdered sugar 1 cup (250 ml) at a time, beating well after each addition, until icing reaches frosting consistency.

CARAMEL BROWNIES

1 (18 OUNCE) SWISS CHOCOLATE CAKE MIX	1 (520 G)
1 (14 OUNCE) PACKAGE CARAMELS	1 (420 G)
1 CUP EVAPORATED MILK, DIVIDED	250 ML
¾ CUP BUTTER, MELTED	180 ML
1 CUP SEMI-SWEET CHOCOLATE CHIPS	250 ML
1 CUP CHOPPED PECANS OR WALNUTS	250 ML

◆ Preheat oven to 350° (176° C).

◆ In large bowl, combine cake mix, butter and ½ cup (125 mL) evaporated milk. Beat on low speed to blend. Spread half of batter into bottom of greased 9 x 13-inch (23 x 33 cm) baking pan.

◆ Bake for 8 minutes. Remove from oven and cool slightly (about 15 minutes).

◆ While cake is baking in medium saucepan, melt caramels in remaining ½ cup (125 mL) evaporated milk over low heat, stirring constantly until mixture is smooth. Remove from heat and set aside.

◆ Sprinkle chocolate chips evenly over cake surface. Pour caramel mixture over chocolate chips and sprinkle nuts over caramel.

◆ Drop remaining batter by spoonsful over nuts and caramel and swirl gently.

◆ Return to oven for 18 to 20 minutes. Cool and refrigerate at least 1 hour before serving.

Whip Up
Some More . . .
Sweets

Here's the section where you'll find all the fabulous desserts that didn't quite fit into the cake, cookies or bars categories. I've included an assortment of desserts, including pies, crunches and various other delights. These recipes don't necessarily use a cake or cookie mix either. These use everything from gelatin and pudding mixes to flavored instant oatmeal. (You've got to try the Cranberry-Apple Crumb on page 218. It's absolutely one of my favorite and most frequently requested recipes.)

PIÑA COLADA CHILLED PIE

This pie has an unbelievably smooth, creamy texture and tastes just like a Piña Colada. If you really like the taste of rum, splash a few extra tablespoons in for some added punch.

1 MEDIUM BANANA, THINLY SLICED	**1**
1 (6 OUNCE) PREPARED GRAHAM CRACKER PIECRUST	**1 (170 G)**
2 (3 OUNCE) PACKAGES COCONUT CREAM INSTANT PUDDING MIX	**2 (85 G)**
¾ CUP COCONUT MILK (NOT CREAM OF COCONUT)	**180 ML**
1 (8 OUNCE) CAN CRUSHED PINEAPPLE WITH JUICE	**1 (228 G)**
⅓ CUP RUM	**80 ML**
1 (8 OUNCE) CONTAINER NON-DAIRY WHIPPED TOPPING	**1 (228 G)**
¼ CUP SHREDDED COCONUT	**60 ML**

◆ Place banana slices in bottom of piecrust.

◆ In large mixing bowl, combine pudding mix, coconut milk, pineapple and rum. Blend on low speed until thoroughly mixed.

◆ Fold in whipped topping and mix well. Pour mixture over bananas in piecrust and sprinkle coconut over top, if desired.

You can generally find coconut milk in the Asian foods section of most grocery stores. I tried this recipe with regular milk and it doesn't have the same texture or flavor. The coconut milk gives it a velvety, creamy texture and adds to the coconut flavor.

MOCHA S'MORES PIE

½ CUP SOUR CREAM	125 ML
1 CUP MILK CHOCOLATE CHIPS	250 ML
1 (9 OUNCE) PREPARED GRAHAM CRACKER PIECRUST	1 (240 G)
1 (14 OUNCE) CAN SWEETENED CONDENSED MILK	1 (420 G)
1 (8 OUNCE) PACKAGE CREAM CHEESE, SOFTENED	1 (228 G)
2 TABLESPOONS INSTANT COFFEE GRANULES	30 ML
1 CUP MILK	250 ML
1 (6 OUNCE) INSTANT CHOCOLATE PUDDING MIX	1 (170 G)
1 ½ CUPS MARSHMALLOW CREAM	375 ML

◆ In small saucepan, melt chocolate with sour cream over low to medium heat, stirring constantly until mixture is smooth and well blended.

◆ Pour into piecrust and use back of spoon to smooth chocolate mixture evenly over bottom and sides of crust. Refrigerate to set chocolate while you prepare filling.

◆ In medium mixing bowl, combine sweetened condensed milk and cream cheese. Blend on low speed.

◆ Dissolve coffee granules in milk and add to cream cheese mixture while continuing to blend on low speed.

◆ While beating, slowly add pudding mix. Beat for 1 to 2 minutes. Pour mixture into piecrust and smooth top. Refrigerate until chilled (about 1 hour).

◆ Heat marshmallow cream on half power in microwave to soften and smooth over chocolate pie filling. Keep pie refrigerated until ready to serve.

Add the marshmallow cream topping just before serving each piece or it will slide off pie as it sits.

MANDARIN ORANGE-CHOCOLATE PIE

This easy pie looks and tastes like orange sherbet. It makes a great summer dessert.

1 (11 OUNCE) CAN MANDARIN ORANGES WITH LIGHT SYRUP	1 (312 G)
½ CUP WATER	125 ML
1 (3 OUNCE) PACKAGE ORANGE INSTANT GELATIN	1 (85 G)
1½ CUPS (1 PINT) WHIPPING CREAM	375 ML
1 CUP SUGAR	250 ML
1 (8 OUNCE) PACKAGE CREAM CHEESE, SOFTENED	1 (228 G)
1 TEASPOON VANILLA	5 ML
1 (1 OUNCE) SQUARE SEMI-SWEET BAKING CHOCOLATE, MELTED, COOLED	1 (28 G)
1 (9 OUNCE) PREPARED GRAHAM CRACKER PIECRUST	1 (240 G)

◆ Drain ½ cup (125 mL) syrup from mandarin oranges. In small pan, heat water and orange syrup. Stir in gelatin until it dissolves. Remove from heat and cool.

◆ Beat whip cream until peaks form; set aside.

◆ Cream sugar, cream cheese and vanilla. Pour gelatin mixture into cheese and sugar mixture and blend well. Fold in whip cream.

◆ Remove 1 cup (250 mL) mixture and stir in chocolate. Pour into piecrust and smooth.

◆ Place in freezer for 10 to 15 minutes or until firm. Gently stir oranges into remaining mixture; pour over chocolate. Refrigerate for several hours until firm or until ready to serve.

For a decorative effect, beat remaining whipping cream with 1 tablespoon powdered sugar and use for garnish.

CHOCOLATE-PEANUT BUTTER PIE

¾ CUP MILK CHOCOLATE CHIPS	180 ML
4 TABLESPOONS WHIPPING CREAM	60 ML
1 (3 OUNCE) PACKAGE CREAM CHEESE, SOFTENED	1 (85 G)
½ CUP CREAMY PEANUT BUTTER	125 ML
1 (5 OUNCE) COOK-AND-SERVE VANILLA PUDDING MIX	1 (142 G)
1¾ CUPS MILK	430 ML
1 (6 OUNCE) PREPARED CHOCOLATE PIECRUST	1 (170 G)

◆ In small saucepan, melt chocolate chips, cream over low heat and stir until well blended. Remove from heat.

◆ In medium saucepan, combine cream cheese, peanut butter, vanilla pudding mix and milk; bring to a boil, stirring frequently. Remove from heat and cool for 10 to 15 minutes.

◆ Pour half of pudding mixture in piecrust and smooth over. Spread half of chocolate mixture over pudding and top with remaining pudding mixture.

◆ Use a butter knife to swirl chocolate through pudding mixture to create marbled effect.

◆ Take remaining chocolate and pour evenly over top. Cool and place pie in refrigerator until ready to serve.

CHOCOLATE-ALMOND PUDDING PIE

The pudding mix used in this pie and the versions that follow give each its own unique flavor. These pies are very similar in nature to pecan pies; the nuts (and coconut) bake on the surface, making a thin crust over the pie filling beneath.

1 (4 OUNCE) CHOCOLATE COOK-AND-SERVE PUDDING MIX	1 (115 G)
1 CUP LIGHT CORN SYRUP	250 ML
¾ CUP EVAPORATED MILK	180 ML
1 EGG, SLIGHTLY BEATEN	1
1 TEASPOON ALMOND EXTRACT	5 ML
1 CUP COARSELY CHOPPED PECANS	250 ML
1 (6 OUNCE) PREPARED CHOCOLATE PIECRUST	1 (170 G)

◆ Preheat oven to 375° (190° C). In medium bowl, blend pudding mix with corn syrup. Gradually add evaporated milk, egg and almond extract, stirring until well blended.

◆ Stir in pecans and pour mixture into piecrust.

◆ Bake for 40 minutes (just until top begins to crack). Remove from oven and cool for several hours. (Pie will jiggle slightly in middle when you remove it from oven.) If desired, serve with dollop of whipped cream.

(CONTINUED ON NEXT PAGE.)

(CONTINUED)

VARIATIONS OF PUDDING PIES

COCONUT PIE:

1 (3 OUNCE) VANILLA COOK-AND-SERVE PUDDING MIX	1 (85 G)
1 CUP LIGHT CORN SYRUP	250 ML
¾ CUP EVAPORATED MILK	180 ML
1 EGG, SLIGHTLY BEATEN	1
1 CUP SHREDDED COCONUT	250 ML
1 (6 OUNCE) PREPARED GRAHAM CRACKER PIECRUST	1 (170 G)

◆ Prepare according to directions for *Chocolate-Almond Pudding Pie* on page 214.

CASHEW-TOFFEE PIE:

1 (4 OUNCE) CHOCOLATE COOK-AND-SERVE PUDDING MIX	1 (115 G)
1 CUP LIGHT CORN SYRUP	250 ML
¾ CUP EVAPORATED MILK	180 ML
1 EGG, SLIGHTLY BEATEN	1
¾ CUP CRUSHED TOFFEE PIECES	180 ML
½ CUP COARSELY CHOPPED CASHEWS	125 ML
1 (6 OUNCE) PREPARED GRAHAM CRACKER PIECRUST	1 (170 G)

◆ Prepare according to directions for *Chocolate-Almond Pudding Pie* on page 214 and stir in toffee pieces and cashews.

TURTLE PIE

This rich, wonderful pie combines the favorite flavors of chocolate and caramel, just like the turtle candy.

7 OUNCES INDIVIDUALLY WRAPPED CARAMELS	
(ABOUT 22 PIECES)	**198 G**
¼ CUP EVAPORATED MILK	**60 ML**
¾ CUP CHOPPED PECANS, DIVIDED	**180 ML**
2 (3 OUNCE) PACKAGES CREAM CHEESE,	
SOFTENED	**2 (85 G)**
½ CUP (4 OUNCES) SOUR CREAM	**125 ML**
1¼ CUPS MILK	**310 ML**
½ CUP SUGAR	**125 ML**
1 (4 OUNCE) PACKAGE CHOCOLATE	
INSTANT PUDDING MIX	**1 (115 G)**
1 (6 OUNCE) PREPARED GRAHAM	
CRACKER CRUST	**1 (170 G)**
½ CUP CHOCOLATE SYRUP OR FUDGE TOPPING	**125 ML**

◆ In medium saucepan, combine caramels and evaporated milk. Cook over medium heat for 5 minutes, stirring constantly.

◆ Remove from heat. Stir in ½ cup (125 mL) chopped pecans. Pour mixture into piecrust.

◆ In medium bowl, combine cream cheese, sour cream, milk and sugar. Blend until mixture is smooth.

◆ Add pudding mix and blend for about 30 seconds more, until pudding mix is well incorporated.

◆ Spoon mixture over caramel in piecrust. Refrigerate for about ½ hour or until set.

◆ Drizzle chocolate syrup or spoon fudge topping over pie. Sprinkle with remaining pecans. Keep refrigerated.

APPLE-CRUMB PIE

*This pie is another family favorite. To save
time I usually use a frozen pie shell.*

5 TO 7 MEDIUM GRANNY SMITH APPLES	**5 TO 7**
1 (6 OUNCE) UNBAKED PIECRUST	**1 (170 G)**
½ CUP SUGAR	**125 ML**
2 (2 OUNCE) CINNAMON-SPICE	
INSTANT OATMEAL PACKETS	**2 (57 G)**
½ CUP FINELY CHOPPED PECANS	**125 ML**
⅓ CUP FLOUR	**80 ML**
⅓ CUP PACKED BROWN SUGAR	**80 ML**
⅓ CUP BUTTER, MELTED	**80 ML**

◆ Preheat oven to 400° (204° C). Pare apples, slice into eighths and arrange in unbaked piecrust. Sprinkle sugar evenly over apples.

◆ In medium bowl, combine oatmeal, pecans, flour and brown sugar and mix well.

◆ Add melted butter to mixture and blend thoroughly (mixture should be crumbly).

◆ Place mixture on top of apples and bake for 35 to 40 minutes or until top is brown.

CRANBERRY-APPLE CRUMB

*Although I usually serve this as a side dish, it works
just as well as a dessert. It has been requested at
family gatherings for years and is now a staple of our
Thanksgiving and Christmas dinners. Be sure to buy
extra packages of cranberries around the holidays
when they're plentiful and freeze them to enjoy this
delicious dish throughout the year. (I just put the bagged
cranberries in the freezer and thaw them before using.)*

4 CUPS GRANNY SMITH APPLES, PEELED, CHOPPED	1 L
2 CUPS FRESH CRANBERRIES	500 ML
2 TABLESPOONS FLOUR	30 ML
1 CUP SUGAR	250 ML
3 (2 OUNCE) CINNAMON-SPICE INSTANT	
OATMEAL PACKETS	3 (57 G)
¾ CUP CHOPPED PECANS	180 ML
½ CUP FLOUR	125 ML
½ CUP PACKED BROWN SUGAR	125 ML
½ CUP BUTTER, MELTED	125 ML

◆ Preheat oven to 350° (176° C). In large bowl, combine apples, cranberries and 2 tablespoons (30 mL) flour. Toss to coat.

◆ Add sugar and mix well. Put mixture into ungreased 2-quart (2 L) casserole dish.

◆ Combine oatmeal, pecans, ½ cup (125 mL) remaining flour, brown sugar and butter. Stir well and spoon over apple mixture.

◆ Bake uncovered for 45 minutes or until topping is well browned.

AMARETTO-PEACH CRUNCH

*Like a peach pie with a crunchy topping (the cake mix
and almonds form a crust over the pie filling as this
bakes), the only way to enhance this dessert is to serve
it with a big scoop of vanilla ice cream on the side.*

2 (21 OUNCE) CANS PEACH PIE FILLING	**2 (598 G)**
½ CUP AMARETTO LIQUEUR	**125 ML**
1 (18 OUNCE) WHITE CAKE MIX	**1 (520 G)**
1 CUP BLANCHED, SLIVERED ALMONDS	**250 ML**
½ CUP (1 STICK) BUTTER	**125 ML**

◆ Preheat oven to 350° (176° C). Spread pie filling evenly in
bottom of greased 9 x 13-inch (23 x 33 cm) baking pan. Pour
amaretto over filling.

◆ Sprinkle cake mix evenly and smooth top. Sprinkle almonds
evenly over cake mix.

◆ Slice butter into ⅛-inch slices and place over entire surface. Bake
for 40 to 45 minutes until top is brown.

BLUEBERRY CRUNCH

It's pretty hard to visualize how this dish will turn out until you make it yourself. (This version was a big hit with my husband's co-workers.) If you like the taste of blueberry, you'll love this dessert.

1 (20 OUNCE) CAN CRUSHED PINEAPPLE WITH JUICE	1 (570 G)
½ CUP PACKED BROWN SUGAR	125 ML
1 TEASPOON CINNAMON	5 ML
1 (21 OUNCE) CAN BLUEBERRY PIE FILLING	1 (598 G)
1 (18 OUNCE) YELLOW CAKE MIX	1 (520 G)
1 CUP CHOPPED PECANS	250 ML
½ CUP (1 STICK) BUTTER	125 ML

◆ Preheat oven to 350° (176° C). Grease 9 x 13-inch (23 x 33 cm) baking pan. Pour pineapple and juice into pan and spread evenly.

◆ Sprinkle brown sugar and cinnamon over top.

◆ Drop blueberry pie filling over pineapple and smooth over gently.

◆ Sprinkle cake mix evenly over pie filling and sprinkle pecans over cake mix.

◆ Slice butter into ⅛-inch pieces and distribute over surface. Bake for 50 to 55 minutes or until light brown on top.

BANANA-CREAM DELIGHT

¾ CUP (1 ½ STICKS) BUTTER, SOFTENED	180 ML
1 ½ CUPS FLOUR	375 ML
⅔ CUP FINELY GROUND WALNUTS	180 ML
1 (8 OUNCE) PACKAGE CREAM CHEESE, SOFTENED	1 (228 G)
1 CUP POWDERED SUGAR	250 ML
1 (8 OUNCE) CONTAINER FROZEN WHIPPED TOPPING	1 (228 G)
3 CUPS MILK	750 ML
2 (3 OUNCE) PACKAGES BANANA CREAM INSTANT PUDDING	2 (85 G)
2 BANANAS	2

◆ Preheat oven to 350° (176° C). In medium bowl, cream butter and flour. Add walnuts and blend thoroughly.

◆ Press into bottom of ungreased 9 x 13-inch (23 x 33 cm) baking dish. Bake for 30 minutes and cool.

◆ Mix cream cheese with powdered sugar, add 4 ounces (115 g) frozen topping and blend. Spread mixture over cooled crust.

◆ In medium bowl, whisk milk and pudding mix for 2 minutes. Pour over cheese mixture.

◆ Slice bananas and place on top of pudding. Carefully spread remaining 4 ounces (115 g) frozen whipped topping over all. Refrigerate for several hours before serving.

TWO-TONED CHOCOLATE CHEESECAKE

You can eat this cheesecake as is (it just melts in your mouth) or spoon some cherry pie filling or strawberries in syrup over each slice just before serving. It's a really pretty dessert; the darker chocolate cheesecake layer contrasts with the white cheesecake layer beneath, which sits atop a cookie-like crust.

1 (18 OUNCE) YELLOW CAKE MIX	1 (520 G)
¼ CUP VEGETABLE OIL	60 ML
3 EGGS, DIVIDED	3
1 ¼ CUPS MILK CHOCOLATE CHIPS, DIVIDED	310 ML
3 (8 OUNCE) PACKAGES CREAM CHEESE, SOFTENED	3 (228 G)
½ CUP SUGAR	125 ML
½ CUP SOUR CREAM	125 ML
½ CUP WHIPPING CREAM	125 ML

◆ Preheat oven to 350° (176° C). Reserve 1 cup (250 mL) dry cake mix and set aside.

◆ To prepare crust, put remaining cake mix, oil and 1 egg in large bowl. Beat on low speed until dough forms.

◆ Add ½ cup (125 mL) chocolate chips and blend into mixture.

(CONTINUED ON NEXT PAGE.)

(CONTINUED)

◆ Press dough into bottom of greased, floured 9 x 13-inch (23 x 33 cm) baking pan. Bake for 10 minutes.

◆ While crust is baking, prepare cheesecake filling. In large bowl (the same one you made crust in is fine), beat cream cheese until smooth and creamy.

◆ Add 2 eggs, one at a time, beating well after each addition.

◆ Add reserved cake mix, sugar, sour cream and whipping cream. Beat on low speed to blend, then beat on medium speed for 3 minutes, until mixture is light and fluffy.

◆ Reserve 2 cups (500 mL) cheese mixture and spoon remaining mixture over hot, baked crust.

◆ Melt remaining ¾ cup (180 mL) chocolate chips and blend into reserved cheese mixture. Spoon chocolate cheese mixture carefully over cheese mixture in pan.

◆ Bake for 30 to 35 minutes until edges are set. Don't overcook. Cool to room temperature and refrigerate before serving.

SPICY APPLE TART

This dish is not only tasty, but also very pretty.
The apples and custard-like filling make an
attractive topping for the spicy, sweet base.

1 (18 OUNCE) SPICE CAKE MIX	1 (520 G)
½ CUP CHOPPED WALNUTS	125 ML
½ CUP (1 STICK) BUTTER, SOFTENED	125 ML
¼ CUP PLUS 2 TABLESPOONS SUGAR, DIVIDED	60 ML
1 TEASPOON CINNAMON	5 ML
1 CUP SOUR CREAM	250 ML
1 EGG	1
3 GRANNY SMITH OR BAKING APPLES, PEELED, CORED, THINLY SLICED	3
½ CUP CHOPPED DATES	125 ML

◆ Preheat oven to 350° (176° C). In large bowl, combine cake mix, walnuts and butter. Blend on low speed until butter is thoroughly incorporated (mixture will be crumbly).

◆ Press mixture into bottom and one fourth of way up sides of greased, floured 9 x 13-inch (23 x 33 cm) baking pan. Bake for 10 minutes.

◆ While crust is baking, mix cinnamon in small bowl with ¼ cup (60 mL) sugar until well blended. Set aside.

◆ In separate bowl, blend sour cream with egg and remaining 2 tablespoons (30 mL) sugar.

◆ Remove crust from oven. Distribute apple slices and dates evenly over bottom. Sprinkle cinnamon-sugar mixture over top. Spoon sour cream mixture on top. Bake for 35 to 40 minutes.

BANANA-CHOCOLATE TREAT

1 (18 OUNCE) YELLOW CAKE MIX	**1 (520 G)**
½ CUP (1 STICK) BUTTER, SOFTENED	**125 ML**
2 CUPS SEMI-SWEET CHOCOLATE CHIPS	**500 ML**
4 CUPS MILK, DIVIDED	**1 L**
4½ CUPS MINIATURE MARSHMALLOWS, DIVIDED	**1 L 125 ML**
2 LARGE BANANAS, SLICED	**2**
2 (3 OUNCE) PACKAGES VANILLA INSTANT	
PUDDING MIX	**2 (85 G)**
1 CUP FROZEN WHIPPED TOPPING, THAWED	**250 ML**
1½ CUPS SHREDDED COCONUT, DIVIDED	**375 ML**

◆ Preheat oven to 350° (176° C). In large bowl, combine cake mix with butter; blend until mixture is crumbly. Press into bottom of greased 9 x 13-inch (23 x 33 cm) baking dish. Bake for 10 minutes. Remove from oven and cool.

◆ In large saucepan, combine chocolate chips, 1 cup (250 mL) milk and 2 cups (500 mL) marshmallows. Cook over low heat, stirring constantly until marshmallows melt. Pour mixture over cooled crust. Chill for about 1 hour.

◆ Place banana slices in single layer over chocolate mixture.

◆ In medium bowl, whisk pudding mix with 3 cups (750 mL) milk. Whisk in whipped topping. Stir in remaining marshmallows and 1 cup (250 mL) coconut.

◆ Spoon over bananas. Sprinkle remaining coconut over top. Keep refrigerated.

PISTACHIO-MARSHMALLOW DESSERT SALAD

*With its pale green color, this salad adds a nice touch
of color to any meal. (I always think it looks festive
next to the red color of cranberry sauce around
the holidays, but it also works well throughout
the year used as either a dessert or side dish.)*

1 (3 OUNCE) PACKAGE PISTACHIO INSTANT PUDDING MIX	1 (85 G)
1 (8 OUNCE) CONTAINER FROZEN WHIPPED TOPPING	1 (228 G)
1 (20 OUNCE) CAN CRUSHED PINEAPPLE WITH JUICE	1 (570 G)
1 CUP CHOPPED PECANS	250 ML
1 ½ CUPS MINIATURE MARSHMALLOWS	375 ML
½ CUP SHREDDED COCONUT	125 ML

◆ In large bowl, combine pudding mix and whipped topping; stir until well blended.

◆ Add pineapple, pecans, marshmallows and coconut. Stir well. Refrigerate until ready to serve.

FUN-FUDGE SHAPES

This is a fun and EASY candy recipe that uses pudding mix as a basic ingredient. It's a great way to make special holiday-shaped candies using mini cake pans. You can whip up a batch in less than 10 minutes and have them ready to serve the next hour.

½ CUP (1 STICK) BUTTER	125 ML
½ CUP MILK	125 ML
2 (3 OUNCE) PACKAGES CHOCOLATE COOK-AND-SERVE	
PUDDING MIX	2 (85 G)
1 (1 POUND) BOX POWDERED SUGAR	1 (454 G)
1 CUP MINIATURE MARSHMALLOWS	250 ML
½ CUP CHOPPED PECANS	125 ML

◆ In heavy, medium saucepan, combine butter, milk and pudding mix. Heat to simmer and cook for 2 minutes, stirring constantly.

◆ Remove from heat and stir in powdered sugar until well blended, then stir in marshmallows and pecans.

◆ Spoon mixture into greased miniature cake pan. (I especially like using pans with holiday shapes. For instance, around Valentine's Day, I like to use a pan that has six small heart shapes. Each are a few inches wide and about 1¼ inch deep. This recipe is enough to make 6 of them.)

◆ Refrigerate until firm. Turn out of pan and serve.

FESTIVE PUMPKIN TREAT

1 (17 OUNCE) OATMEAL COOKIE MIX	1 (487 G)
1 (8 OUNCE) PACKAGE CREAM CHEESE, SOFTENED	1 (228 G)
2 TABLESPOONS ORANGE LIQUEUR OR MILK	30 ML
2 TABLESPOONS SUGAR	30 ML
2 CUPS FROZEN WHIPPED TOPPING, THAWED	500 ML
1 CUP COLD MILK	250 ML
1 (16 OUNCE) CAN PUMPKIN	1 (454 G)
2 (3.4 OUNCE) PACKAGES VANILLA INSTANT PUDDING MIX	2 (100 G)
1 TEASPOON CINNAMON	5 ML
¼ TEASPOON GROUND GINGER	1 ML
⅛ TEASPOON GROUND CLOVES	.5 ML

TOPPING:

½ CUP CHOPPED PECANS	125 ML
2 TABLESPOONS BUTTER	30 ML
⅓ CUP PACKED BROWN SUGAR	80 ML

◆ Preheat oven to 375° (190° C). Prepare cookie batter according to package directions. Press cookie batter into bottom of greased 9 x 13-inch (23 x 33 cm) baking pan. Bake for 10 to 12 minutes or until light brown. Remove from oven and cool.

◆ While cookie crust is baking, prepare toppings. In medium bowl, combine cream cheese with orange liqueur and sugar. Beat on medium until mixture is smooth. Fold in whipped topping. Set aside.

◆ In large bowl, combine milk with pumpkin, pudding mixes, cinnamon, ginger and cloves. Beat with whisk until well blended.

◆ Spread pumpkin mixture over cooled crust and smooth over top. Carefully cover with cream cheese mixture and smooth.

◆ If you want to serve this with topping, mix pecans, butter and brown sugar in small bowl. Sprinkle over slices just before serving.

◆ This sets up fairly quickly, but for best results, refrigerate for several hours.

CHUNKY CHOCOLATE CANDY

1 (3 OUNCE) PACKAGE CHOCOLATE COOK-AND-SERVE	
PUDDING MIX	**1 (85 G)**
1 CUP SUGAR	**250 ML**
½ CUP PACKED BROWN SUGAR	**125 ML**
½ CUP EVAPORATED MILK	**125 ML**
1 TABLESPOON BUTTER	**15 ML**
1 CUP CHOPPED PECANS	**250 ML**
½ CUP SHREDDED COCONUT	**125 ML**
½ CUP RAISINS	**125 ML**

◆ In heavy medium saucepan, combine pudding mix, sugar, brown sugar, milk and butter.

◆ Cook over medium heat until sugar dissolves and mixture comes to a boil.

◆ Continue cooking, stirring frequently, until mixture reaches softball stage 237° F or (114° C) on candy thermometer (about 7 minutes).

◆ Remove from heat and stir in pecans, coconut and raisins. Beat well and before mixture starts to harden (work fast), drop by heaping spoonsful onto wax paper.

Several recipes throughout this book are perfect for one holiday or another. Sometimes I've pointed this out in the recipes, but I by no means covered them all. So, to make it easy to see all of the recipes that would be especially good for one holiday or another, we've listed them here in this handy chart.

Strawberry-Bundt Cake, p. 77
Red Velvet Cake, p. 98
Strawberry-Cream Cheese Bars, p. 197
Black Forest Cherry-Cake Brownies, p. 203
Black Forest Cherry Cookies, p. 148
Valentine's Day Cheery-Cherry Cookies, p. 159

Key Lime Pie Cake, p. 36
Watergate Cake, p. 76
Pina Colada Chilled Pie, p. 210
Pistachio-Marshmallow Dessert Salad, p. 226

Anisette Easter Cake, p. 58
Pretty Pastel Easter Cookies, p. 159
Pistachio-Marshmallow Dessert Salad, p. 226

Watermelon Cake with Lime Frosting, p. 101
Blueberry Crunch, p. 220

Halloween Orange-Chocolate Cookies, p. 158
Mandarin Orange-Chocolate Pie, p. 212

THANKSGIVING

CHRISTMAS

TERMS YOU'LL WANT TO KNOW
(Tools and Terminology)

BAKING PANS

The baking pans used for the cake recipes in this book are mostly limited to the following three: rectangular baking pan, round cake pans and bundt pan.

Round cake pans come in a couple of different sizes and materials. The ones used for making the recipes in this book were 8¼ x 2-inch glass pans. Glass and dark-colored pans absorb more heat than shiny metal ones and make the cakes brown more quickly, so you'll need to take this into account when using your own. You may need to extend the cooking time slightly if you're using metal pans.

Some other common sizes are 8 x 1½ inches, 9 x 1½ inches and 9 x 2 inches. For the recipes in this book, 9 x 1½ inches or 9 x 2 inches would work just fine.

Rectangular baking pans come in several different sizes also, but the one used in this book is a 13 x 9 x 2-inch metal pan, which is probably the most common. If you're using a larger size, you'll want to check the cake for doneness a few minutes before the cooking time specified in the recipe to make sure your cake isn't over baking. You'll also want to check a little earlier if you're using a glass pan, since glass pans make baked goods cook faster.

Bundt pans are traditionally 10 inches wide, 3½ inches deep and holds 12 cups (3 L). The hole in the middle of this tube pan with fluted sides provides for even heating and cooking.

BEAT

When the recipe says to "beat" the ingredients, you use an electric mixer (usually set to medium speed) or by hand. 100 strokes by hand roughly equals 1 minute by electric mixer.

CREAM

To cream ingredients means to beat them until the mixture is soft, smooth and "creamy". Frequently a recipe will specify creaming butter and sugar or cream cheese and sugar.

When creaming 2 or more ingredients, the end result should be a uniformly smooth mixture, where none of the individual ingredients are identifiable anymore.

Depending upon the quantity of ingredients that needs to be blended, I usually use a fork for small quantities and an electric mixer for larger batches.

CUT-IN

Cutting-in ingredients refers to the way you mix butter with dry ingredients, using a knife or pastry blender, until the mixture is crumbly. You'll use this technique when making the crumb toppings called for in several recipes in this book.

FOLD

Folding an ingredient into a recipe is done when you're combining a light, airy mixture (like beaten egg whites) with a heavier mixture (such as cake batter).

To do this, place the lighter mixture on top of the heavier one in a large bowl. Starting at the back of the bowl, use a rubber spatula to cut down vertically through the two mixtures, across the bottom of the bowl and up the nearest side.

Rotate the bowl slightly with each series of strokes. You should use a gentle motion and continue until the mixtures combine.

DOUBLE BOILER

Used in recipes that need indirect, gentle heat to melt ingredients or cook some frostings (like 7-Minute Frosting). A double boiler is made up of two pots—one is designed to fit snugly over the other, leaving enough room to put several inches of water in the bottom.

If you don't have a double boiler, you can easily make one by putting a large metal bowl over a pot of simmering water, without letting the water touch the bowl.

GREASING AND FLOURING

Greasing and flouring your cake pans is critical for successful baking. You don't want half of your cake to stick to the pan when you go to turn it out onto a serving tray.

For best results, use solid shortening (like Crisco). Using a small piece of wax paper or paper towel, spread a thin layer of shortening over the entire interior surface of the pan.

Dust the pan by placing about 1 tablespoon flour inside and shaking it around until the entire surface is coated. Dump out the remaining flour and fill the pan with batter.

JELLY-ROLL PAN

Jelly-roll pans are shallow, rectangular baking pans with 1 inch sides (much like a cookie sheet). They come in several sizes, but the most common is 15½ x 10½ x 1 inches. They are used, as the name implies, for making jelly-rolls as well as cakes and some bars. This is the pan used in the *Colossal Petits Fours* recipe in this book because of its shallow depth, which makes a cake just the right height for cutting with a cookie cutter.

PASTRY BLENDER

This useful tool is designed for cutting butter into flour (or a flour mixture). It's fitted with 5 or 6 U-shaped, rigid, curved wires and easily slices butter into small pieces (without melting it) to mix with the flour. You'll want to have this for recipes that require a crumb topping (like *Cranberry-Apple Crumb*).

Spatula

A spatula is a flat, narrow utensil, made from plastic or metal, that comes in several sizes and is used for spreading icings. In this book, I've referred to it as an "icing spatula" to distinguish it from a rubber scraper, also called a spatula.

A rubber scraper (spatula) is great for scraping liquid ingredients and batters out of bowls and utensils. It helps ensure that all of your ingredient goes into the recipe or pan (and also makes cleanup easier too).

A turner, also frequently called a spatula, is what you typically use to flip pancakes. These are also used to lift cookies from a baking sheet. They come in both metal and plastic.

If you're using non-stick cookie sheets, be sure to use a plastic spatula/turner so you don't scratch the surface of your pan.

WHISK

A wire whisk consists of a series of looped wires fastened at the top by a long handle. They are used to whip air into ingredients such as egg whites or whipping cream.

They're also great for getting a smooth consistency in some icing recipes. They come in many sizes and it's useful to have a couple. I have a very small one and a large one and use both all the time.

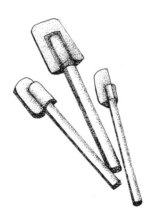

SEPARATING EGGS

When you separate eggs, cleanly remove the yolk from the white. There are a couple of methods for doing this.

1) Method 1—Take a dry egg in your hand and tap it firmly across the wide end of the shell on the rim of the bowl.

   Holding the widest part in your hand, pull the shells apart. The widest end becomes the "cup" that will hold the yolk, as the white drips into the bowl.

   Pour the yolk into the other shell, continuing to let the white drip into the bowl and repeat until all the white drains and the yolk is left. Dump the yolk into another bowl or container.

   Inspect the whites to be sure that no shell fragments fell in with them.

2) Method 2—Use a yolk separator, which is designed for this purpose. (I frankly haven't used a yolk separator, but believe if you want to take extra precautions with regard to minimizing the risk of contamination from salmonella germs on the shells, you may want to use one. Since the eggs used in the cake batter are cooked, I don't think it's necessary to worry about it though.)

Did You Know? Cold eggs separate easier than those at room temperature.

YOUR INGREDIENTS

BUTTER

Made from churned cream, butter by law is at least 80% milk fat with water and some milk solids making up the remaining 20%.

STORAGE
Butter should be its stored in the refrigerator and covered, since it picks up other food flavors. (Don't store it next to foods with strong odors like onions or garlic.)

You can keep it for up to 2 weeks, but should use it before the expiration date printed on the package.

You can also freeze butter for up to 4 months. Seal it in a plastic bag for best results.

SUBSTITUTIONS
If necessary, you can use unsalted butter instead of salted (or vice versa) if that's what you have on hand. You don't need to worry about adding additional salt to your recipe if you use unsalted.

Whipped butter can be used in the place of stick butter as well, but be sure to substitute the amount you need by weight, not volume. For example, if the recipe requires 1 cup (2 sticks) (250 mL) butter (which is half a pound), you'll want to use 8 ounces (228 g) whipped butter.

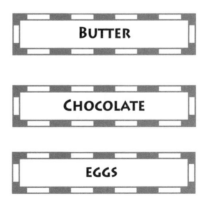

BUTTER

CHOCOLATE

EGGS

Cutting-In Butter

When a recipe says to "cut-in butter", this means to mix cold butter with the other ingredients by gently pressing a pastry blender or cutter into the butter and flour mixture until the mixture is crumbly and looks like coarse meal.

Creaming

When a recipes calls for "creaming the butter", it means to beat the butter until it's soft, smooth and creamy. You can do this by hand with a food processor or with an electric hand mixer. It's much easier to do this if the butter is at room temperature and not cold.

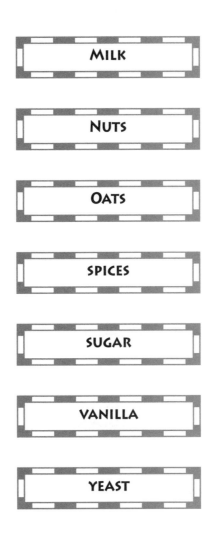

MILK

NUTS

OATS

SPICES

SUGAR

VANILLA

YEAST

CHOCOLATE

My favorite ingredient! Chocolate is made from cocoa beans which are processed to obtain cocoa butter and a dark brown paste called "liquor". Once dried, the liquor is ground into the powder known as unsweetened cocoa.

Chocolate comes in many forms: bars, chips, chunks, cocoa powder, etc. and it's helpful to know a little about the ones that may be called for in a recipe. Here's a rundown of the most commonly used forms required for recipes in this book.

- Unsweetened baking chocolate, frequently used as bars or squares, contains chocolate liquor (the substance extracted from the hulled beans) and between 50% and 58% cocoa butter.

- Bittersweet chocolate, usually called for in squares or bars, contains at least 35% chocolate liquor, sugar and vanilla.

- Semi-sweet and sweet chocolate, which comes in baking chips, bars or squares, contains between 15% and 35% chocolate liquor, sugar and vanilla.

- Milk chocolate, frequently called for as chips or squares, contains 10% chocolate liquor, sugar, vanilla and at least 12% milk solids.

- Unsweetened cocoa is cocoa liquor dried and ground into powder.

Did You Know? White chocolate is not "true chocolate" because it contains no chocolate liquor, but is instead prepared from sugar, cocoa butter, milk solids and vanilla.

STORAGE

Keep chocolate stored tightly wrapped in a plastic bag in a cool, dry location. The ideal storage temperature is around 75° (24° C). If chocolate is stored at a high temperature, it may turn grayish (this is called "bloom" and is a result of the fat content surfacing). Go ahead and use it anyway. This discoloration is perfectly harmless.

Unsweetened, bittersweet and semi-sweet chocolate, if properly stored, can stay fresh for very long periods of time.

Unsweetened dry cocoa powder will keep indefinitely if stored in a cool, dry location.

Don't store milk chocolate and white chocolate for longer than 9 months, because they contain milk solids.

SUBSTITUTIONS

You can use bittersweet and semi-sweet chocolate interchangeably in recipes, but you may notice some slight differences in flavor and texture.

If you don't have unsweetened cocoa but do have Dutch-processed cocoa, you can go ahead and use it instead, although the flavor will be milder.

1 ounce (28 g) semi-sweet chocolate = 3 tablespoons (45 mL) semi-sweet chocolate pieces or 1 ounce (28 g) unsweetened chocolate plus 1 tablespoon (15 mL) sugar.

1 ounce (28 g) unsweetened chocolate = 3 tablespoons (45 mL) unsweetened cocoa plus 1 tablespoon (15 mL) melted butter.

1 ounce (28 g) sweet baking chocolate= 2 tablespoons (30 mL) unsweetened cocoa plus 4 teaspoons (20 mL) sugar and 2 teaspoons (10 mL) butter.

SUBSTITUTION "DON'TS"

Don't use chocolate syrup in place of melted chocolate. (Use it only when specifically called for.)

Instant cocoa mix is not the same as unsweetened cocoa. It contains milk powder and sugar and may affect the flavor of your baked goods.

MELTING CHOCOLATE

Melt chocolate in the microwave, over direct heat or over hot water in double boiler.

To microwave: Use a microwave-safe bowl and set the power to medium (or half-power) and heat for short periods of time (30 to 45 seconds) stirring occasionally until chocolate melts.

To melt over direct heat: Place chocolate in pan over very low heat. Be careful when melting over direct heat, chocolate scorches easily. You'll want to heat it very slowly and stir it frequently.

To melt over hot water using a double boiler: Heat the chocolate slowly over hot, not boiling, water (as steam can stiffen or harden it).

Note: Be sure to cool the melted chocolate to about 80° before adding it to your recipe.

Did You Know? Chocolate comes from cocoa beans that grow in pods on a tropical "Theobroma cacao" tree, cultivated mainly in South American countries.

EGGS

Eggs are used to not only add flavor and color, but also to tenderize and provide structure for your baked goods. Both brown and white eggs contain the same flavor and nutritional value.

STORAGE

Eggs should always be refrigerated and stored in their original carton, if possible, which will help keep them from absorbing refrigerator odors.

You can store eggs for up to 5 weeks beyond the packing or expiration date on the carton, as long as they are not cracked or broken.

SUBSTITUTIONS

There are some substitutions that can be made for eggs.

1 whole egg = 2 egg whites. (Be aware that they won't provide the same flavor and texture, however.)

¼ cup (60 mL) liquid egg substitute = 1 whole egg. Egg substitutes contain egg whites, nonfat milk, vegetable oils and other ingredients to replace the yolk. If you use egg substitutes in a cake recipe, for example, your end result may not be as tender or rich.

1 egg white = 1 tablespoons (15 mL) meringue powder plus 2 tablespoons (30 mL) water. You can use powdered egg whites in most recipes that call for egg whites.

BEATING EGG WHITES

For best results when beating egg whites, make sure no traces of broken yolk get into the whites. Make sure your bowl and beaters don't have any traces of fat on them, which can prevent the whites from expanding to their full volume when beaten. (To ensure you don't have any fat on the utensils, you can rinse them in a solution of water and some vinegar.)

It's best to bring egg whites to room temperature for 20 minutes after you've separated them from the yolks. This will help the egg whites beat to their highest volume.

Select clean, fresh eggs which have been handled properly and refrigerated.

Don't use cracked or leaking eggs that may have a bad odor or unnatural color when cracked open. They may have been contaminated with salmonella and it's better not to take the chance.

Use large eggs unless a recipe specifies a different size.

Cold eggs are easiest to separate.

Did You Know? You can easily test an egg for freshness by placing it in a bowl deep enough to cover it with cold water. If the egg stays on the bottom of the bowl, it's fresh. If it stands up and bobs on the bottom, it isn't as fresh. If it floats, you need to throw it away!

MILK AND CREAM

Here's a little information about the different kinds of milk products called for in cake and icing recipes.

- Whole milk has no fat removed and contains 3½% milk fat.
- Buttermilk traditionally was the liquid remaining after butter was churned. Today it is made by adding a culture to low-fat or non-fat milk, which gives it a thick texture and tangy flavor.
- Half-and-half is a mixture of milk and cream and contains between 10.5% and 18% milk fat.
- Evaporated milk is milk that has had 60% of its water removed.
- Sweetened condensed milk has 50% of the water removed. The remaining mixture is 40% sugar and very sticky and sweet.
- Whipping cream is skimmed from milk that has been standing 24 hours or longer. It's usually classified as either light, meaning it has 30 to 36% milk fat or heavy, meaning it contains from 36% to 40% milk fat.
- Half-and-half is a mixture of milk and cream that contains about 10% to 18% milk fat.

STORAGE

Store milk products in their original containers in the refrigerator at a temperature of 35° to 40° (2° to 4° C).

You can store unopened cans of evaporated milk or sweetened condensed milk at room temperature for up to 12 months. Once you open it, however, refrigerate the unused portion in an airtight container for up to 5 days.

It's best not to freeze milk, cream, buttermilk, evaporated milk or sweetened condensed milk because the texture will be affected.

SUBSTITUTIONS
Whole milk, reduced fat and fat-free milk can be used interchangeably in recipes.

1 cup (250 mL) buttermilk = 1 tablespoon (15 mL) vinegar or lemon juice in a measuring cup with enough milk to equal 1 cup (250 mL). Let stand 5 minutes before using.

1 cup (250 mL) refrigerated fresh milk = ½ cup (125 mL) evaporated milk plus ½ cup (125 mL) water.

1 cup (250 mL) whipping cream = ¾ cup (180 mL) milk and ⅓ cup (80 mL) butter. (Don't use this for to make whipped cream; use only for baking.)

One 14-ounce (420 g) can sweetened condensed milk = 1 cup (250 mL) instant nonfat dry milk, ⅔ cup (160 mL) granulated sugar, ½ cup (125 mL) boiling water and 3 tablespoons (45 mL) melted butter. Beat in a blender or food processor until smooth.

SUBSTITUTION DON'TS
Don't use evaporated milk in place of sweetened condensed milk.

NUTS

Nuts add flavor and a crunchy texture to baked products. They are actually the edible kernel of a dried fruit contained inside a hard shell. The most commonly used nuts called for in recipes within this book include walnuts, pecans and almonds.

You can purchase them chopped, whole or still within the shells to shell them yourself. Most of the recipes will specify chopped or ground nuts. If you're buying them already chopped, be aware that 1 cup (250 mL) chopped nuts equals 4 ounces (115 g).

STORAGE

Store shelled nuts in an airtight container in a cool place. Because of their high fat content, nuts can go rancid very quickly. Heat, light and moisture also make nuts go rancid faster.

You can refrigerate shelled nuts for up to 4 months or freeze them for up to 6 months. Unshelled nuts can be kept about twice as long.

SUBSTITUTIONS

Often you can substitute the same quantity of a different nut than called for in the recipe with perfectly fine results.

USAGE

When you choose shelled nuts, look for those that are crisp in texture and uniform in color. Don't buy them if they are shriveled or discolored.

To be sure they are fresh before you use them, it's always best to taste them before adding them to your recipe.

OATS

Oats add a chewy texture and a nutty flavor to baked products. You'll notice that there are several kinds of dried oats on the market.

Old-Fashion Oats: The entire oat kernel is rolled to make old-fashion rolled oats.

Quick-Cooking Oats: The oat kernel is cut into pieces before being rolled thinly to make quick-cooking oats.

Instant Oatmeal: The oats are cut very fine and processed so that no cooking is necessary other than adding boiling water. Instant oatmeal is often flavored with sugar and spices.

STORAGE
Store oats in a cool dry place in a tightly covered container, to keep out dust, moisture and insects for up to 6 months.

You can also freeze oats for up to 1 year in a plastic freezer bag.

Although they don't go bad, oats may become stale with age.

SUBSTITUTIONS
Old-fashion and quick-cooking oats can be used interchangeably.

Do not, however, use instant oatmeal instead of old-fashion or quick-cooking oats. Because it usually contains sugar and other flavors, instant oatmeal can alter the texture and taste of your recipe.

SPICES

Spices, which are obtained from the bark, buds, fruit, roots, seeds or stems of a variety of plants, have been prized for centuries for their pungent aroma and ability to flavor foods. Herbs are harvested mainly from the leafy parts of plants .

Many popular baking spices include allspice, cardamom, cinnamon, cloves, ginger and nutmeg, which are available both in whole or ground form. The recipes in this book all use ground spices.

STORAGE
Spices should be stored in airtight containers in a cool, dark location for about 6 months. When exposed to heat, light and moisture, spices can lose their flavor more quickly. Do not store spices above the range or oven.

SUBSTITUTIONS
1 teaspoon (5 mL) ground allspice = ¼ teaspoon (1 mL) ground cinnamon, ½ teaspoon (2 mL) ground cloves and ¼ teaspoon (1 mL) ground nutmeg, mixed together.

1 teaspoon (5 mL) ground cinnamon: ½ teaspoon (2 mL) ground allspice or 1 teaspoon (5 mL) ground cardamom.

1 teaspoon (5 mL) ground ginger = ½ teaspoon (2 mL) ground mace plus ½ teaspoon (2 mL) grated lemon peel.

1 teaspoon (5 mL) ground nutmeg = 1 teaspoon (5 mL) ground allspice or 1 teaspoon (5 mL) ground cloves or 1 teaspoon (5 mL) ground mace.

USAGE
Because they quickly lose their aroma and flavor, it's best to buy ground spices in small amounts.

SUGAR

In addition to adding sweetness, sugar also tenderizes and helps baked goods to brown.

Granulated white sugar is refined cane or beet sugar. It's what's intended in all the recipes that don't specify a particular type of sugar (e.g. brown sugar or powdered sugar).

Powdered (or confectioner's) sugar is granulated sugar ground to a fine powder with cornstarch added to prevent it from clumping. It provides smoothness for recipes, such as those for icings, where granulated sugar would be too grainy.

Brown sugar is granulated sugar with molasses added to it and it comes in 2 types. Light brown sugar has a more delicate flavor than its counterpart dark brown sugar. Unless dark brown sugar is specified in the recipe, use light brown sugar. (Although you're probably safe using either for most of the recipes in this book.)

STORAGE
Store granulated sugar tightly covered in a cool, dry location. (A moist location, like a refrigerator, can cause clumping.)

Brown sugar and powdered sugar should be stored in either a plastic bag or airtight container.

Although sugars don't go bad, they can sometime harden or form lumps when exposed to moisture.

SUBSTITUTIONS
1 cup (250 mL) granulated sugar = ¾ cup (180 mL) honey (but reduce the liquid in the recipe by ¼ cup (60 mL)).

1 cup (250 mL) granulated sugar = ½ cup (125 mL) corn syrup.

1 cup (250 ml) powdered sugar = 1 cup (250 mL) granulated sugar plus ⅛ teaspoon (.5 mL) cornstarch (process on high speed in a food processor until it has a fine texture).

1 cup (250 mL) light brown sugar = 1 cup (250 mL) granulated sugar plus 2 tablespoons (30 mL) molasses.

Usage

Here are a few tips for properly measuring sugar to ensure best results.

Granulated sugar: Spoon sugar into a measuring cup and level with a spatula or knife.

Powdered sugar: Lightly spoon sugar into dry measuring cup and level top with a spatula or knife.

Brown sugar: Pack brown sugar firmly into a dry measuring cup.

Did You Know? To soften brown sugar that has hardened you can do one of 2 things:

1) Put brown sugar in a container, cover with a piece of foil or plastic wrap and place a crumpled, damp paper towel on the foil or wrap. Cover tightly and let sit. (The sugar will absorb the moisture from the paper towel and become soft.)

2) The faster method: Put an open bag of brown sugar in the microwave and set 1 cup (250 mL) water next to it. Microwave on high power (100%) for 2 to 3 minutes, but stop frequently to check your progress, until brown sugar softens.

VANILLA EXTRACT

Vanilla extract adds a very sweet, fragrant flavor to baked goods. It is produced from the long, thin pods harvested from an orchid native to tropical America. It has been cultivated and processed for hundreds of years.

Vanilla extract is produced by processing vanilla beans in an alcohol and water mixture and then aging it for several months.

STORAGE
Store vanilla extract in a cool, dark place with the bottle tightly closed to prevent evaporation and loss of flavor. Vanilla extract will stay fresh for years if stored properly.

SUBSTITUTIONS
You can use imitation vanilla in the place of real vanilla extract, as is sometimes necessary with certain recipes, although it's not optimal. It doesn't have the same flavor and the imitation vanilla can actually have an artificial taste.

Some of the recipes in this book call for using imitation vanilla when real vanilla would discolor the end result (for instance, in a white, sugar glaze). If the recipe doesn't specify "clear" vanilla, use the real thing!

USAGE
When measuring vanilla, it's a good idea not to measure over your mixing bowl to avoid accidentally spilling more than you need into your recipe.

YEAST

Yeast is a living, plant-like, single-cell microscopic organism that is activated by warm liquid. As it feeds on sugar or starch it grows and multiplies, releasing carbon dioxide as it grows, the gas that causes baked products to rise and produces a light texture in the finished bread product.

There are several forms of yeast on the market.
- Active dry yeast, the most popular form, is sold as dry granules in .25 ounce (7 g) packets or 4-ounce (115 g) jars. The recipes in this book call for the .25 ounce (7 g) packets, although you can use the equivalent amount measured from the jar (see "Substitutions" below).
- Quick-rising yeast is a more active strain of yeast than regular active dry yeast and can reduce the rising time by one-third.
- Compressed fresh yeast is a small block or "cake" of moist yeast found in the refrigerated section of the supermarket. It is very perishable and should be used within 1 to 2 weeks of purchase or by the expiration date printed on the package.

STORAGE
Packets of dry yeast and quick-rising yeast need to be stored in cool, dry location to keep out moisture. Once opened, however, it's best to store jars of yeast tightly covered in the refrigerator.

Tightly wrapped compressed yeast can be stored in the refrigerator and used by the expiration date printed on the package. It can also be frozen in a plastic bag for up to 3 months. (If compressed yeast gets moldy or discolors, you should throw it out.)

SUBSTITUTIONS

Quick-rising dry yeast can be substituted for active dry yeast.

One (.6 ounce) cake compressed yeast = 1 (.25 ounce) (7 g) packet of active dry yeast.

2½ teaspoons (12 mL) active dry yeast = 1 (.25 ounce) (7 g) packet active dry yeast.

USAGE

For best results, let dough rise at a temperature between 70 to 85° (21° to 29° C).

When dissolving yeast in water, make sure the water temperature is between 105° and 115° (41° to 46° C). You want it warm enough to activate the yeast, but not hot enough to kill it.

You should also test or "proof" your yeast before using it to be sure it's still active. To do this, dissolve the amount of yeast to be used in your recipe in the amount of warm water specified in the recipe and add a pinch of sugar.

Set the mixture aside in a warm place for 5 to 10 minutes. If it starts to foam and expand, the yeast is alive and active.

Did you know? Each .25 ounce (7 g) dry yeast envelope contains thousands of yeast cells.

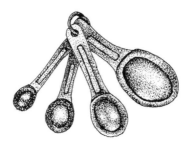

EQUIVALENTS

FOOD	QUANTITY	YIELD
Almonds, sliced	2¼ ounces (65 g)	½ cup (125 mL)
Almonds, slivered	2 ounces (57 g)	⅓ cup (80 mL)
Apple pie filling	21-ounce can (598 g)	2⅓ cups (580 mL)
Apples, fresh	1 medium	¾ cup chopped (180 mL); 1 cup diced or sliced (250 mL)
Apples, fresh	1 pound (454 g)	3 medium; 2½ cups peeled (750 mL), diced or sliced; 3 cups unpeeled (750 mL), diced or sliced
Apple slices, canned	20-ounce can (570 g)	2 drained
Apricots, canned	16-ounce can (454 g)	2 cups drained halves (500 mL); 6 to 8 whole
Apricots, dried	6-ounce package (170 g)	1 cup dried (250 mL); 2 cups cooked (500 mL)
Apricots, fresh	2 medium	½ cup sliced (125 mL)
Apricots, fresh	1 pound (454 g)	2 cups halves or slices (500 mL); 8 to 12 medium
Baking powder	7-ounce can (198 g)	1¼ cups (310 mL)
Baking soda	16-ounce box (454 g)	2⅓ cups (580 mL)
Bananas, dried, sliced	1 pound (454 g)	4 to 4½ cups (1 L to 1 L 125 mL)

EQUIVALENTS

FOOD	QUANTITY	YIELD
Bananas, fresh	1 medium	1 cup sliced (250 mL)
Bananas, fresh	1 pound (454 g)	3 small or large; 1½ cups mashed (375 mL); 2 cups sliced (500 mL)
Bisquick	40-ounce box (1.13 kg)	12 cups (3 L)
Blueberries, canned	15-ounce can (438 g)	1½ cups (375 mL)
Blueberries, fresh or frozen	1 pound (454 g)	3½ cups (875 mL); makes 1 (9 inch) pie (23 cm)
Blueberry pie filling	21-ounce can (598 g)	2⅓ cups (580 mL)
Butter	2 tablespoons (30 mL)	"the size of a walnut"
Butter	¼-pound stick (115 g)	½ cup (125 mL); 8 tbsp.; 1 stick; 12 to 16 pats; ⅓ cup clarified butter (80 mL)
Butter	½ pound (228 g)	25 servings
Butter	1 pound (454 g)	2 cups; 4 sticks (500 mL)
Butter, soft	8-ounce tub (228 g)	1 cup (250 mL)
Butter, whipped	1 pound (454 g)	3 cups (750 mL)
Butterscotch morsels	12-ounce package (340 g)	2 cups (500 mL)

EQUIVALENTS

FOOD	QUANTITY	YIELD
Cake mix	18-ounce box (520 g)	5 to 6 cups batter (1.5 L); 2 (9-inch round) layers (23 cm); 2 (8-inch square) layers (20 cm); 1 (13 x 9 x 2 inch) cake (33 x 23 cm); 1 cartoon character cake; 24 cupcakes
Cake, sheet (9 x 13 inch)	1½ cakes	25 servings
Cake, two layer (9 inch)	2 to 2½ cakes	25 servings
Cherries, canned, tart	16-ounce pitted (454 g)	1½ cups drained (375 mL)
Cherries, dried, tart	3-ounce package (85 g)	½ cup (125 mL)
Cherries, fresh, sweet	1-pound unpitted (454 g)	1 quart (1 L); 1¾ cups (430 mL)
Cherries, frozen, tart	1-pound pitted (454 g)	2 cups (500 mL)
Cherry pie filling	21-ounce can (598 g)	2⅓ cups (580 mL)
Chocolate, bar or square	1 ounce (28 g)	3 tablespoons (45 mL) chopped or grated
Chocolate, bar or square	9 ounces (240 g)	1⅝ cups chopped or grated (435 mL); 1 cup (250 mL)

EQUIVALENTS

FOOD	QUANTITY	YIELD
Melted chocolate, unsweetened	1 ounce (28 g)	1 square; 4 tablespoons grated (60 mL)
Chocolate, unsweetened	1 ounce (28 g)	1 envelope liquid
Chocolate bits, M&M's	12-ounce package (340 g)	1½ cups (375 mL)
Chocolate kisses (mini)	10-ounce package (284 g)	209 pieces
Chocolate morsels	12-ounce package (340 g)	2 cups (500 mL)
Chocolate wafers	20 wafers	1 cup fine crumbs (250 mL)
Cinnamon, ground	1 ounce (28 g)	4 tablespoons (60 mL)
Cinnamon, stick	1-inch part of stick	1 teaspoon ground (5 mL)
Cocoa, baking	8-ounce tin	2⅔ cups (660 mL)
Coconut, flaked	3½-ounce can (100 g)	1¼ cups (310 mL)
Coconut, flaked	7-ounce package (198 g)	2½ cups (625 mL)
Coconut, flaked	14-ounce package (420 g)	5⅓ cups (1 L, 330 mL)
Coconut, fresh	1 pound (454 g)	1 medium; 3 cups grated or chopped (750 mL)
Crackers, graham	15 (2½-inch square)	1 cup fine crumbs (250 mL)
Crackers, graham, crumbs	3¾ cups (930 mL); 13½-ounce box (460 g)	makes 3 pie shells

EQUIVALENTS

FOOD	QUANTITY	YIELD
Cranberries, fresh	12-ounce package (340 g)	3 cups (750 mL)
Cranberries, fresh	1-pound package (454 g)	4 cups (1 L); 3 cups cooked sauce (750 mL)
Cream, heavy	½ pint (500 mL)	1 cup unwhipped (250 mL); 2 cups whipped (500 mL)
Cream, heavy (unwhipped)	¾ pint (750 mL)	25 servings
Cream, light (half-and-half)	1 pint (500 mL)	2 cups (500 mL); 16 coffee servings
Cream, whipped, pressurized	7-ounce can (198 g)	1⅞ cups (465 mL)
Cream cheese	3-ounce package (85 g)	⅓ cup (80 mL)
Cream cheese	8-ounce package (228 g)	1 cup (250 mL)
Dates, diced, sugared	1 pound (454 g)	2⅔ cups (680 mL)
Dates, dried, pitted	8-ounce package (228 g)	54 dates; 1¼ cups chopped (310 mL)
Dates, dried with pits	1 pound (454 g)	60 dates; 2½ cups pitted (625 mL)
Flour, all-purpose	5-pound bag (2.5 kg)	20 cups sifted (5 L)
Flour, cake	1 pound (454 g)	4⅛ cups unsifted (1L); 4⅝ cups sifted (1 L, 125 mL)
Flour, self-rising	1 pound (454 g)	4 cups sifted (1 L)

EQUIVALENTS

FOOD	QUANTITY	YIELD
Ginger, crystallized	1 tablespoon (15 mL)	1 teaspoon ground (5 mL)
Ginger, fresh	1 tablespoon chopped (15 mL)	1 teaspoon ground (5 mL)
Ginger, fresh	1½ to 2-inch piece	2 tablespoons grated or chopped (30 mL)
Ginger, ground	½ teaspoon (2 mL)	1 teaspoon fresh chopped (5 mL)
Ginger, ground	1 ounce (28 g)	4 tablespoons (60 mL)
Lemons	1 pound (454 g)	4 to 6 medium; ⅔ to 1 cup juice (160 to 250 mL)
Macadamia nuts	7-ounce jar (198 g)	1½ cups (375 mL)
Marshmallow cream	7-ounce jar (198 g)	2⅛ cups (530 mL)
Milk	1 quart (1 L)	4 cups (1 L)
Milk, sweetened, condensed	14-ounce can (420 g)	1¼ cups (310 mL)
Mincemeat	27-ounce jar (800 g)	2⅔ cups (560 mL)
Mincemeat, condensed	9-ounce box (240 g)	½ cup (125 mL)
Molasses	12-ounce bottle (340 g)	1½ cups (375 mL)
Oreo cookies	12 cookies	1 cup fine crumbs (250 mL)
Oreo cookies	1 pound, 4 ounce package (570 g)	51 cookies

EQUIVALENTS

FOOD	QUANTITY	YIELD
Peaches, canned, sliced	16-ounce can (454 g)	2 to 2½ cups drained (500 to 625 mL)
Peaches, fresh	1 pound (454 g)	3 to 4 medium; 2 cups peeled and sliced or diced (500 mL); 1½ cups pulp (375 mL)
Peaches, fresh	2 pounds (1 kg)	makes 1 (9-inch) pie (23 cm)
Peaches, frozen	10 ounces (284 g)	1 cup slices drained (250 mL); 1¼ cups sliced with juice (310 mL)
Peach pie filling	21-ounce can (300 g)	2⅓ cups (580 mL)
Pecans, chips or pieces	6-ounce package (170 g)	1½ cups (375 mL)
Raisins, seedless	1-pound package (454 g)	3 cups (750 mL)
Raspberries, fresh	1 pint (500 mL)	1¾ cups (430 mL)
Raspberries, frozen	10-ounce package (284 g)	1 cup with syrup (250 mL)
Shortening, solid	1-pound can (454 g)	2½ cups (625 mL)
Shortening, sticks	20-ounce package (570 g)	3 sticks, 1 cup each (250 mL)
Strawberries, fresh	1 cup whole (250 mL)	4 ounces (115 g); ½ cup pureed (125 mL)
Strawberries, fresh	1 pint (500 mL)	2½ cups whole (625 m L); 1¾ cups sliced (430 mL); 1¼ cups pureed (310 mL); 12 large, 24 medium or 36 small

EQUIVALENTS

FOOD	QUANTITY	YIELD
Strawberries, frozen, sliced	10-ounce package (284 g)	1 cup drained (250 mL); 1¼ cups with syrup (310 mL)
Strawberries, frozen, whole	20-ounce package (570 g)	4 cups whole (1 L); 2¼ cups pureed (560 mL)
Strawberry pie filling	21-ounce can (578 g)	2⅓ cups (680 mL)
Sugar, brown	1 pound (454 g)	2¼ cups packed (560 mL)
Sugar, confectioners	1 pound (454 g)	3¾ cups unsifted (930 mL); 4¼ cups sifted (1 L, 60 mL)
Sugar, granulated	1 pound (454 g)	2¼ cups (560 mL)
Sugar, granulated	5-pound bag (2.5 kg)	11¼ cups (3 L)
Sugar cubes	1-pound box (454 g)	96 cubes
Vanilla extract	1 ounce (28 g)	2½ tablespoons (37 mL)
Vanilla wafers	30 wafers	1 cup fine crumbs (250 mL)
Walnuts, halves	7-ounce package (198 g)	1¾ cups (430 mL)
Walnuts, pieces	2½-ounce package (71 g)	½ cup (125 mL)
Whipped topping, frozen	8-ounce carton (228 g)	3½ cups (875 mL)
Whipped topping mix	1.4-ounce package (35 g)	2 cups whipped topping (560 mL)

SUBSTITUTION LIST

IF YOU NEED THIS:
>SUBSTITUTE THIS

2 tablespoons (30 mL) almonds, ground (for flavoring):
>¼ teaspoon (1 mL) almond extract

1 teaspoon (5 mL) apple pie spice:
>½ teaspoon (2 mL) ground cinnamon plus
>¼ teaspoon (1 mL) ground nutmeg plus
>⅛ teaspoon (.5 mL) ground allspice plus
>⅛ teaspoon (.5 mL) ground cardamom

1 teaspoon (5 mL) baking powder, double acting:
>¼ teaspoon (1 mL) baking soda plus
>½ cup (125 mL) buttermilk
>(Reduce other liquid in recipe by ½ cup (125 mL).)

2¼ cups (560 mL) biscuit mix:
>2 cups (500 mL) flour, sifted with plus
>1 tablespoon (15 mL) baking powder
>1 teaspoon (5 mL) salt plus
>¼ cup (60 mL) shortening (cut in)

1 cup (250 mL) butter (for baking):
>⅞ cup (220 mL) shortening plus
>½ (2 mL) teaspoon salt

1 cup (250 mL) buttermilk:
>1 tablespoon (10 mL) lemon juice or white vinegar plus
>⅞ cup (220 mL) plus 1 tablespoon (15 mL) whole milk
>(Let stand for 10 minutes.)

1 cup (250 mL) buttermilk (for baking):
>1 cup (250 mL) plain yogurt or 1 cup (250 mL) sour cream

6 ounces (170 g) chocolate morsels:
>9 tablespoons (135 mL) cocoa powder plus
>7 tablespoons (105 mL) sugar plus
>3 tablespoons (45 mL) butter

SUBSTITUTION LIST

IF YOU NEED THIS:

SUBSTITUTE THIS

2 ounces (57 g) chocolate, semisweet:

⅓ cup (80 mL) chocolate chips

1 ounce (28 g) chocolate, semisweet:

½ ounce (14 g) unsweetened chocolate plus

1 tablespoon (15 mL) sugar

1 ounce (28 g) chocolate square, unsweetened:

3½ tablespoons (52 mL) cocoa powder plus

2 teaspoons (10 mL) butter or shortening

1 cup (250 mL) grated coconut:

1⅓ (330 mL) cups flaked coconut

1 cup (250 mL) heavy cream (for cooking, not whipping):

¾ cup (180 mL) whole milk plus

⅓ cup (80 mL) butter

1 cup (250 mL) light cream:

½ cup (125 mL) heavy cream plus

½ cup (125 mL) whole milk

1 cup (250 mL) light cream (for cooking):

⅞ cup (220 mL) whole milk plus

3 tablespoons (45 mL) butter

1 cup (250 mL) light cream (for cooking):

1 cup (250 mL) evaporated milk

1 cup (250 mL) cream, whipped, sweetened:

4 ounces (115 g) whipped topping

1 cup (250 mL) cream, whipped, sweetened:

1¼ ounces (35 g) dessert topping mix, prepared

1 cup (250 mL) whipping cream:

⅔ cup (160 mL) evaporated milk plus

4 teaspoons (20 mL) lemon juice or vinegar

SUBSTITUTION LIST

IF YOU NEED THIS:
>SUBSTITUTE THIS

1 cup (250 mL) whipping cream:
>½ cup (125 mL) nonfat dry milk plus
>⅓ cup (80 mL) water plus
>1 tablespoon (15 mL) lemon juice

1 teaspoon (5 mL) cream of tartar:
>1 teaspoon (5 mL) lemon juice or vinegar

1 cup (250 mL) cake flour, sifted:
>⅞ cup (220 mL) all purpose flour plus
>2 tablespoons (30 mL) cornstarch

1 cup (250 mL) self-rising flour, sifted:
>1 cup (250 mL) all-purpose flour plus
>1½ teaspoons (7 mL) baking powder plus
>¼ teaspoon (1 mL) salt (Mix and substitute measure for
>measure for self-rising flour. Omit any additional
>baking powder and salt called for in recipe.)

1½ cups (375 mL) fruit, fresh, cut up:
>16 ounces (454 g) canned fruit, drained

1¼ cups (310 mL) fruit, fresh, cut up:
>10 ounces (284 g) frozen fruit, drained

1 cup (250 mL) half-and-half:
>⅞ cup (220 mL) whole milk plus
>1½ teaspoons (7 mL) butter

1 cup (250 mL) half-and-half:
>½ cup (125 mL) light cream plus
>½ cup (125 mL) whole milk

1 teaspoon (5 mL) lemon or lime peel, fresh:
>1 teaspoon (5 mL) lemon or lime peel, dried

1 teaspoon (5 mL) lemon or lime peel, fresh (for flavoring):
>½ teaspoon (2 mL) lemon or lime extract

SUBSTITUTION LIST

IF YOU NEED THIS:

SUBSTITUTE THIS

1 cup (250 mL) milk, sweetened, condensed:

1 cup (250 mL) nonfat dry milk plus
½ cup (125 mL) boiling water plus
⅔ cup (160 mL) sugar plus
3 tablespoons (45 mL) melted butter
(Process mixture in blender until smooth.)

1 cup (250 mL) milk, evaporated:

1 cup (250 mL) cream

1 cup (250 mL) milk, whole:

½ cup (125 mL) evaporated milk plus
½ cup (125 mL) water

8 cups (2 L) piecrust mix:

6¼ cups (1.5 L) flour, mixed with plus
1 tablespoon (15 mL) salt plus
2½ cups (625 mL) shortening (cut in)

1 cup (250 mL) sour cream (for baking):

¾ cup (180 mL) sour milk or buttermilk plus
⅓ cup (80 mL) butter

1 cup (250 mL) sour cream (for baking):

1 cup (250 mL) plain yogurt plus
1 teaspoon (5 mL) baking soda

METRIC CONVERSION

Here is a simple chart that makes conversion from
U.S. measurements to metric as easy as pie.

1 teaspoon	5 ml
2 teaspoons	10 ml
1 tablespoon	15 ml
2 tablespoons	30 ml
1 cup	237 ml
2 cups = 1 pint	473 ml
3 cups	710 ml
4 cups = 1 quart	.95 liter
4 quarts = 1 gallon	3.8 liters
1 ounce	28 grams
2 ounces	57 grams
3 ounces	85 grams
4 ounces	113 grams
6 ounces	170 grams
8 ounces	228 grams

OVEN TEMPERATURES

FAHRENHEIT	DESCRIPTION	CELSIUS
200°	Very cool	95°
225°	Cool	110°
250°	Very slow	120°
300°	Slow	150°
325°	Warm	165°
350°	Moderate	175°
375°	Moderately hot	190°
400°	Hot	200°
450°	Very hot	230°
500°	Extremely hot	260°

INDEX

271

Cheese Frosting 89
Butterscotch Bars 184
Cherry-Almond Bars 173
Cherry Cake 100
Cherry Cheese Squares 220
Cherry Cordial Cake 68
Cherry Strudel 39
Chocolate-Oatmeal Cake 26
Chocolate-Topped Toffee Bars 182
Coconut Cake 73
Colossal Petit Fours 118
Cookies and Cream Layer Cake 114
Fuzzy Caterpillar Cake 82
Key Lime Pie Cake 36
Maple-Iced Walnut Cookies 152
Marbled Banana-Chocolate Layer Cake 86
Pineapple-Macadamia Nut Bars 198
Pineapple Torte 108
Pineapple-Upside-Down Cake 47
Pumpkin-Rum Cake 52
Raspberry Rum-Raisin Cake 50
Red Velvet Cake 98
Strawberry-Bundt Cake 77
Strawberry-Lemon Cake with Fluffy
    Cream Cheese Frosting 28
Watergate Cake 76
Watermelon Cake with Lime Frosting 101
White Chocolate Bundt Cake 80
White Chocolate Macadamia
    Nut Cookies 139

White Chocolate
Cherry Cake 100
Colossal Petit Fours 118
Lemon-Cheesecake Bars with White
    Chocolate Frosting 192
Never-Ending Chocolate Bundt Cake 66
White Chocolate Bundt Cake 80
White Chocolate Bundt Cake 65
White Chocolate Macadamia
    Nut Cookies 139

Y

Yellow Cake Mix
Apple Cider Bundt Cake 75
Apple-Cranberry Streusel 38
Apple Crumb Cake 40
Apple Coffee Cake 78
Applesauce Cake with Praline Topping 21
Apricot-Brandy Cake 57
Apricot-Oatmeal Bars 191
Apricot-Streusel Bundt Cake 74
Banana-Chocolate Treat 225
Banana Layer Cake with Butter-
    Pecan Frosting 90
Banana-Nut Cake 29
Blueberry Cream Cheese Cake 63

Blueberry Crunch 220
Cinnamon Rolls 120
Cool and Fruity Lemon Cake 22
Cream Cheese Filled Coffee Cake Rolls 122
Fluffy Orange Cake 24
Lemon-Raspberry Crumb Bars 172
Luscious Orange Torte 102
Marbled Cheesecake Bars 193
Orange-Banana Bundt Cake with
    Buttermilk Glaze 80
Orange-Meringue Torte with
    Apricot Filling 114
Orange-Topped Lemon Bundt Cake 64
Orange-Walnut Coffee Cake 72
Pecan Pie Bars 174
Pineapple-Rum Cake 51
Sticky Buns 124
Two-Toned Chocolate Cheesecake 222

Z

Zucchini Cake with Lemon Cream
    Cheese Frosting 92

MY PERSONAL RECORD

Page #	Recipe Name	Comments

MY PERSONAL RECORD

Page #	Recipe Name	Comments